HEALING WOUNDS

HEALING WOUNDS

ERIK VARDEN

BLOOMSBURY CONTINUUM
LONDON · OXFORD · NEW YORK · NEW DELHI · SYDNEY

BLOOMSBURY CONTINUUM
Bloomsbury Publishing Plc
50 Bedford Square, London, WC1B 3DP, UK
29 Earlsfort Terrace, Dublin 2, Ireland

BLOOMSBURY, BLOOMSBURY CONTINUUM and the Diana logo are trademarks of Bloomsbury Publishing Plc

First published in Great Britain 2024

Copyright © Erik Varden, 2024

Erik Varden has asserted his right under the Copyright, Designs and Patents Act, 1988, to be identified as Author of this work

All rights reserved. No part of this publication may be reproduced or transmitted in any form or by any means, electronic or mechanical, including photocopying, recording, or any information storage or retrieval system, without prior permission in writing from the publishers

Bloomsbury Publishing Plc does not have any control over, or responsibility for, any third-party websites referred to or in this book. All internet addresses given in this book were correct at the time of going to press. The author and publisher regret any inconvenience caused if addresses have changed or sites have ceased to exist, but can accept no responsibility for any such changes

A catalogue record for this book is available from the British Library

Library of Congress Cataloging-in-Publication data has been applied for

ISBN: PB: 978-1-3994-1040-3; eBook: 978-1-3994-1041-0; ePDF: 978-1-3994-1042-7;

2 4 6 8 10 9 7 5 3 1

Typeset by Deanta Global Publishing Services, Chennai, India
Printed and bound in Great Britain by CPI Group (UK) Ltd, Croydon CR0 4YY

To find out more about our authors and books visit www.bloomsbury.com and sign up for our newsletters

In memory of my mother and father

By his wounds we are healed.
Isa. 53.5

Contents

Illustrations   VIII

AFFLICTION   1

TRANSFORMATION   23

    Ad pedes – To the Feet   24

    Ad genua – To the Knees   42

    Ad manus – To the Hands   60

    Ad latus – To the Side   78

    Ad pectus – To the Breast   96

    Ad cor – To the Heart   116

    Ad faciem – To the Face   138

FLOURISHING   157

Notes on the Text   177

Illustrations

The Alexamenos Graffito, Rome	12
Apse mosaic with bejewelled cross from the Basilica of Santa Pudenziana, Rome (© Ivan Vdovin / Alamy Stock Photo)	13
Crucifixion scene from the doors of the Basilica of Santa Sabina, Rome (© Paolo Romiti / Alamy Stock Photo)	14
Detail from the 'Smiling Christ' crucifix, Lérins	17
A stanza from the hymn Crux Fidelis in the Cistercian Hymnal	38
Wall painting of crucified monk from the Abbey of Mogiła, Nowa Huta	174

Affliction

Our wounds are intimate to us. Most of the time we try to keep them out of sight, to nurture, for our own and others' benefit, the illusion that they do not exist. We wish to be, or at least seen to be, hale and healthy.

A wound witnesses to health compromised, sometimes transitionally, to a degree, sometimes for good and utterly.

We can recover from the effects of a wound and effectively conceal its traces with cosmetics, material or metaphorical, yet the impact of the wound remains, fixed in our memory, our consciousness, if not in our physical being.

The interiorization of a wound can make it grow and assume fantastic, even grotesque proportions.

Certain lives are determined by efforts to dissimulate wounds. Such can be the legacy of trauma, especially of trauma sustained early in life, that it seems to acquire an autonomous, ordering force in the forging of a destiny.

A woman or man may feel so defined by a wound that any other circumstance, joyful or sad, appears subservient to it. He or she may be convinced that their life's task is essentially the bearing of this wound, as if it were some sort of Sisyphus's stone, and that a moment's inattention to the task would be fatal.

There can be nobility in such endeavour. Perseverance in the face of grief or misfortune is worthy of honour. But there can also be pathos glacially tinged with intimations of futility as the question lingers: 'What on earth for?'

There are situations in which wounds are put on display. From the beginning of recorded history, we find celebrations of war wounds, for example, emblems of courage and sacrifice wrought, in principle, for a high cause. Entire mythologies have come about in praise of such wounds, to keep them in remembrance.

There is, here, ambiguity, for the root of human conflict is often tawdry. Homer, in the *Iliad*, may praise wounds as godlike (and even envisage the wounding of gods, as when Aphrodite is struck by Diomedes' bronze spear), but at the end of the day what we are faced with is a vision of glorified waste brought about by the rage of a cuckolded husband. And we are brought again to ask: 'What for?'

Wounds are paraded, too, in situations of misery. Beggars exposing wounded limbs in public places were until recently a sight we associated, in the affluent West, with nineteenth-century realist painting or with a generic, unfortunate 'abroad'.

That is so no longer. Destitution is prominently back on our streets. In a way it is good that we should see it. Our social conscience must be mobilized.

Yet something within us rebels, soundly. It simply is not right to reduce a woman, man or child to a wound. It is pathetic when people reduce themselves in this way. A wound has no integrity. It feeds on what was once whole. To present to the world a version of self projected through wounded disfigurement is to show a 'self' defaced that subverts, even obliterates personhood. It is to surrender to inward and thereby to social fragmentation.

Human commerce on such terms easily becomes a manipulating game. Rainer Maria Rilke shows how the game is played out in 'The Poor', a poem that reminds us, as Michael Hoffman has written, that Rilke, for years an assistant to the sculptor Rodin, 'isn't all the twittering of angels, the celebration of fruit, saccharine gallantries to old titled ladies, and perverse animadversions on – mainly against – sex'.[*]

> You had no idea who made up the crowd.
> A stranger found there to be beggars in it
> Conducting transactions
> With outstretched empty hands.
>
> They show to the one arrived from afar
> Their rotting mouths;
> He (who can afford it) may observe
> How scab consumes them.
>
> In their dispersed eyes
> His alien face dissolves.
> They're glad to find him seduced.
> When he speaks, they retch.

This brutal text shows how wounds can become the dehumanizing stuff of trade, used to exact pity, rendering impossible the frank exchange of glances, the fixing of another's eyes that invests an encounter with dignity.

At one level there is fairness. The passing stranger has money to spare, the beggar has nothing to lose. But this

---

[*] From an essay by Hoffman in the April 2008 issue of the journal *Poetry*. Hoffman also translates Rilke's poem, '*Die Bettler*', but I choose to provide my own version here.

complementarity works in material terms only. And a human being is more than a unit of matter. The spirit of such exchange, states Rilke, is one of mutual disgust, reinforcing rather than breaking down barriers. There is no trace here of respect or compassion.

Familiarity blinds us to the ever-present working-out of this dynamic. It takes a traveller from afar to recognize it. But he or she, too, will soon enough integrate the view into a perspective whose edges are blurred by habit.

'The poor you will always have with you,' says Christ in the Gospel as Judas is about to betray him for 30 silver coins.[*] This affirmation, an implicit moral imperative, the statement of a *task*, can become a feather pillow on which our weary conscience sleeps while we simply stop noticing wounds that disfigure and hurt the bodies of persons we meet or the body politic we inhabit.

I wished to establish this realistic view from the outset of a book that proposes to meditate on the wounds Jesus Christ sustained in his sacred passion and on the way in which they enable the healing of ours.

There is a tendency in Christian devotion to prettify, even to idealize, wounds. This tendency is perverse. Human nature, created in the image of God to be like God, is made for wholeness. Here and now we inhabit a world that is wounded, groaning in pangs of deliverance.[†] *We* are wounded, subject to the anomaly which Scripture calls

---

[*] Mt. 26.11.
[†] Cf. Rom. 8.22.

'sin', an existential wasting-sickness that eats away at us not unlike the scab afflicting Rilke's beggars. Sin leaves its mark on our spirit and on our body. It can paralyse our will or lead it astray.

To be fully human is to own this state of affairs. It is to be reconciled to loss and the inevitability of death. But it is no less to remember that our woundedness is of time, and that time will pass.

The Christian Gospel envisages the passage from a frank acknowledgement of wounds to the prospect of definitive healing. It proposes a vista of transformation, 'a new heaven and a new earth' where 'death will be no more, mourning and crying and pain will be no more.' There, the first things will have passed.[*]

The first things, though, must happen first. This affirmation has been from the outset, and will ever remain, the stumbling block of Christianity. The human spirit naturally longs for a salvation able to remove at a stroke whatever causes pain, whatever inflicts wounds. The basic expectation of instantaneous relief is much the same whether our register of hope is digital, political, financial, pharmaceutical, metaphysical or spiritual.

In the Gospel, this hope seems at first sight to be met when the Forerunner, John, points to Christ and exclaims: 'Here is the Lamb of God who *takes away* the sins of the world.'[†] Is that not precisely what I look for – an instance apt to lift the load I bear that weighs me down woundingly,

---

[*] Rev. 21.1, 4.
[†] Jn 1.29.

to take it away and dump it I don't honestly care where, be there a carbon footprint involved, as long as I shall never have to set eyes on it again? Reality, however, does not work like that.

Patient exposure to Christ's work and promise makes us see that expectation of this kind is fatuous. The Lamb of God takes sin away not by brandishing a wand but by picking it up and carrying it.* I in turn am summoned to bear my own load.† In so far as I do this in communion with Christ, a member of his body,‡ I shall find my load reconfigured. It will stay recognizably what it is, but the yoke it represents will be easy, its burden light.§ That which before seemed to crush me will buoy me up. I shall be set in a movement of ascent. A sun will arise out of my darkness with healing in its wings,¶ allowing my wounds, as they heal, mysteriously to flourish.

This paradoxical dynamic, which does not make much sense in empirical terms, is at the heart of what Paul calls 'the logic of the cross'. It is madness to the world, but to

---

*The verb John uses in 1.29, αἴρειν, means 'to pick up and carry', much as the *tollere* of Jerome's Vulgate. The point of Christ's carrying sin is of course to do away with it; but the process is not automatic. We who live in the age of the machine and of the virtual must remember that. Our sin is assumed first, then processed through the passion.
†Cf. Gal. 6.5.
‡Eph. 5.30.
§Cf. Mt. 11.30.
¶Cf. Mal. 4.2.

those who madly determine to construct their existence on its terms a source of power, healing, joy.[*]

The cross is the emblem of the fatal wounding of God-made-man. It is central, literally crucial, to the Christian *kerygma*.

In the earliest of the four Gospels, that of Mark, a text conventionally dated to about 65 AD, Jesus's revelation of his call publicly to suffer and die is made halfway through the narrative, at the end of chapter 8. This passage constitutes a cardinal point on which the story turns. Chapters 9 to 16 are essentially the account of the Lord's 'going up' to Jerusalem, to Calvary.

The 'Gospel of Jesus Christ, the Son of God',[†] we are reminded, cannot be packaged just in terms of moral rearmament and social reform. The good news is focused on a sacrifice that 'must' be undergone,[‡] wounds that must be borne, a death that must be suffered.

In the same breath Jesus makes it clear that suffering and death will not have the last word: 'after three days' he will 'rise again'. 'He said all this quite openly.'[§] There was no secret about it. But so imperious is death in human perception that we find it hard to see beyond it. Christian faith and Christian life are a pedagogy that gradually opens our eyes to the non-finality of woundedness.

---

[*]Cf. 1 Cor. 1.18.
[†]Mk 1.1.
[‡]Mk 8.31.
[§]Mk 8.32.

We are educated in this way of seeing by confronting what frightens us, like the Israelites of old on their way out from Mount Hor during the exodus from Egypt. When poisonous serpents invaded their camp and bit them so that many died, Moses prayed to the Lord and received this counsel: 'Make a fiery serpent, and set it on a pole; and everyone who is bitten shall look at it and live.'[*] Moses did as he was told. 'He made a serpent of bronze, and put it on a pole; and whenever a serpent bit someone, that person would look at the serpent of bronze and live.'[†]

In the Fourth Gospel, Jesus applies this ancient incident to himself, that is, to his impending crucifixion, as a prophetic sign. He tells Nicodemus: 'Just as Moses lifted up the serpent in the wilderness, so must the Son of Man be lifted up, that whoever believes in him may have eternal life.'[‡] John wrote some three decades after Mark, in the nineties of the first century. He had so interiorized the proclamation of the cross that he naturally used it at the outset of his Gospel as a structural theme in his overture, to be orchestrated later.

Paul, another capital early witness, also grounded his preaching in the fact of Christ's crucifixion. He did not waste time on subtle preamble. In the early fifties, 20 years after Calvary and before any of the Gospels had reached final form, he wrote to the Corinthians recalling his arrival among them as an evangelist: 'I did not come proclaiming

---

[*] Num. 21.8.
[†] Num. 21.9.
[‡] Jn 3.14–15.

the mystery of God to you in lofty words or wisdom; I decided to know nothing among you except Jesus Christ, and him crucified.'*

The New Testament's consistent stress on the centrality for Christian life and faith of Christ on the cross cruelly wounded should not make us think that Christians took this message onboard easily, however. Paul admits that the account of Christ crucified was destined to be 'a stumbling block to Jews and foolishness to Gentiles'.[†] In Mark's Gospel, Peter, chief among the Twelve, whose disciple Mark was, responds to Jesus's words about needful suffering indignantly, telling his Master off.[‡] John records Jesus's mystic discourse about 'the kind of death he was to die' only to observe that those who heard him 'did not believe him'.[§]

Such perplexity haunts early Christianity. We find it expressed in both words and images.

As far as we know, the earliest pictorial representation of Christ's crucifixion comes from a graffito carved in plaster near the Palatine Hill in Rome. Its precise date is uncertain, but it was probably made in the early second century. At that time there were Christians about in Rome who had heard the Gospel preached by Peter and Paul. This is what the graffito looks like:

---

[*] 1 Cor. 2.1–2.
[†] 1 Cor. 1.23.
[‡] Mk 8.32.
[§] Jn 12.23–37.

The inscription crudely portrays a human body with a donkey's head. The body is fixed to a cross. In a corner, there is what seems like a Y-shaped *tau* cross. To the left stands a man dressed like a soldier with one hand raised in homage. A caption announces in poorly scripted Greek: 'Alexamenos worships god.'

The image is a caricature. It intends to ridicule the worshipper. The joke is pungent. 'Does he worship a crucified man? You can't be serious. What an ass!'

It is sometimes said that, to appreciate the symbolic charge of the crucifix in ancient times, we moderns should think

AFFLICTION

of a hangman's noose or an electric chair. Such associations are misleading. The gallows and chair were thought up as *humane* means of execution. The cross was designed to cause a maximum of drawn-out anguish. Death by crucifixion was messy and humiliating. Alexamenos is presented in this drawing not just as a fool, but as an indecent gawper.

It took a long time, centuries, for Christians to adopt the image of the Crucified as theirs. When the cross first appears in Christian iconography, as in the apse mosaics of the fourth-century Roman basilicas of the Lateran and Santa Pudenziana, it is as a free-standing bejewelled object without a *corpus*, startling in its abstraction. This motif suggests the Johannine trope of the cross as mysteriously 'glorious'.* Shunned is the human reality of the Crucified's abasement and pain.

*cf. Jn 17.1–5.

The integration of the Calvary scene into Christian visual narration begins about a century later. The earliest extant example is a carved panel on one of the wooden doors leading into the basilica of Santa Sabina on the Aventine in Rome. It is schematic, betraying not an ounce of sentiment. The material crosses are all but hidden by the figures of Christ and the thieves, whose extended hands seem deployed in a deliberate gesture, as if they were performing some sort of Oriental dance. The panel is in any case set so high up on the massive door that even today's observers equipped with sophisticated gadgets struggle to see it clearly. At the time when the door was put up, in the early fifth century, most pilgrims would, I dare say, have noticed little but an outline.

The door of Santa Sabina was designed and carved at a time when the Church was combating a range of dualist, gnosticizing heresies set on driving a wedge between spirit and matter. The important Council of Toledo, convened in the year 400, engaged at length with this matter. It specifically condemned the doctrine of a sect known as Priscillianists after their figurehead Priscillian, a bishop of Ávila. This sect maintained that God in Christ had not truly been incarnate, that the Saviour visited Earth in a heavenly body and that he, through his teaching and merely apparent death, sought to free human souls from imprisonment in flesh.

In response to this anti-incarnational position, the Council of Toledo defined a profession of faith that affirmed the Church's realist Christian belief. It fleshed out the *et incarnatus est* of the Nicene Creed. Regarding the human integrity of Jesus, the Fathers of Toledo stressed that

> his body was neither imaginary nor did it merely have form but had substance. And so he had hunger and thirst and suffered pain and wept and felt every kind of bodily hurt. In the end he was crucified, died and was buried, and rose on the third day; afterwards he spoke with his disciples; he ascended to heaven on the fortieth day. This Son of Man is also named the Son of God; however, the Son of God is God and should not be called a son of man. We truly believe in the resurrection of the human body.

They appended, for good measure, a list of anathemas striking heretical claims, including these:

> If anyone should say or believe that the human Jesus Christ was not assumed by the Son of God, let him be anathema. If anyone should say or believe that the Son of God as God suffered, let him be anathema. If anyone

should say or believe that the human Jesus Christ, as a human, was incapable of suffering, let him be anathema.[*]

Expressed in these texts is an admittedly tortuous attempt to address a tension that was only satisfactorily (from a European Christian point of view) resolved at the Council of Chalcedon half a century later, in 451, when the interaction of Christ's godhead and humanity was subtly defined. This definition especially regards his sacred passion. When the Church considers the crucifixion of the Word made flesh, she must at one and the same time safeguard the impassibility of Christ's divinity and the agony of his sacred humanity. She must vindicate the literal truth of the Gospel while upholding a coherent theology and metaphysic.

At Santa Sabina we see this theological enterprise essayed graphically. The crucifixion panel is loyal to the testimony of the evangelists. At the same time it lets Jesus, twice the size of the ordinary mortals flanking him, appear unaffected. He is nailed to the cross as man but uncompromised as God.

Only once an ecumenical council had established a conceptual framework enabling speech about the Lord's humanity in ways that did not imperil the integrity of his divine nature did Christians begin to engage more freely and imaginatively with Jesus's suffering and with the representation of his wounds.

---

[*]These texts can be found in Denzinger's *Enchiridion symbolorum, definitionum et declarationum de rebus fidei et morum*, 37th edn, ed. Peter Hünermann (Freiburg: Herder, 1991), under the section devoted to the pontificate of Anastasius I, a friend of St Jerome's, nn. 187–208.

AFFLICTION

It is not my purpose to pursue the development by which the crucifixion gradually moved from the periphery to the heart of Christian consciousness.* The movement was realized at different paces, with different emphases east and west, north and south, touching every medium: texts, liturgical rites, mosaics, painting, sculpture, music. To follow this process from antiquity to the High Middle Ages is to see how the schematic cypress-wood carving on the Aventine gradually and gracefully morphed into an affective form of art that culminated in the thirteenth century.

*To do so is fascinating, naturally. Anyone wanting a good guide might consult François Boespflug's *La Crucifixion dans l'art: un sujet planétaire* (Montrouge: Bayard, 2019).

Consider for example this 'Smiling Christ', now in the Cistercian abbey on the isle of Lérins. It invests the Crucified's wounds with extraordinary tenderness.

A contemplative broadening of perception brought a growing assent to vulnerability. One is struck, in comparison, by the poverty of Christian art and reflection on this theme today in the West, which seems stunted in its sensibility. In view of this, it is timely to make of Christ's wounds an object of meditation.

In former times such meditation was prodigious. In what follows I shall draw on one source text in particular, a poem that has accompanied me for most of my adult life. It has its origin within the monastic order to which I belong: that of the Cistercians. For centuries it was attributed to Bernard of Clairvaux (1090–1153). Such was the fame of this incomparable monk and writer that his name attracted, as if by magnetic force, any number of more or less plausible pseudepigrapha.

No-one now believes in Bernardine authorship. Modern scholars think the text's author was a Netherlandish monk born half a century after Bernard's death: Arnulf of Leuven (1200–48). A source note in a fourteenth-century manuscript now kept in Brussels attributes the text to Arnulf.[*] There is no compelling reason for disputing this reference. For the purposes of this book I shall take it for granted.

---

[*] In the Bibliothèque royale de Belgique the document is classed as MS 4459–70, fols. 150r–152v, and dated to the year 1320.

Arnulf was an author of some renown. The *Biographia Cisterciensis* lists him as 'Abbot of Villers, Poet'. It sums up his life with monastic succinctness:

> Arnulf was subprior at Villers in Brabant when in 1240 he was elected abbot. In 1248 he laid down his office in order to devote himself to his meditations and studies, but he died during the course of that same year.[*]

We should be careful not to extrapolate too much from so little. We are justified in surmising, though, that Arnulf was a man of virtue and talent: were he not, his brethren would hardly have elected him abbot. His early resignation suggests his lacking a taste for the business of government. Probably he was an earnest monk elected superior despite himself, longing to return to a simple contemplative quest. The first half of the thirteenth century was a time of intense building work at Villers. Such work takes a heavy toll on whoever is in charge. Abbot Arnulf's enjoyment of regained leisure was cut short by a premature death.

We know Arnulf contributed to the annals of the abbey of Villers, which had been founded from Clairvaux in 1146, during Bernard's abbacy. Arnulf was a competent historian. He is further known to have composed a poetic adaptation of the *Summa of Penitential Cases* by Raymond of Peñafort (1175–1275), the long-lived patron saint of canon lawyers. A casuistic manual in verse! Whatever the readership of

---

[*] From the article on Arnulf von Löwen in the online www.zisterzienserlexikon.de.

this work may have been, one cannot but admire such an idealistic venture.

Arnulf is in our day chiefly remembered as the author of the work that interests us here, a substantial prayer-poem contemplating Christ's crucified body. Its Latin title is *Rhythmica oratio ad unum quodlibet membrorum Christi patientis et a cruce pendentis*. We could translate this as 'A Rhythmic Oration to each of the Members of Christ Suffering and Hanging on the Cross'.

The work combines rigorous form with emotional intensity. Its object is Christ in his passion; but the praying subject is constantly drawn into the text, invited to self-scrutiny. What does Christ's suffering mean for me? How can I make sense of what Paul hints at in Galatians, when he says: 'I have been crucified with Christ; it is no longer I who live, but Christ who lives in me; and the life I now live in the flesh I live by faith in the Son of God, who loved me and gave himself for me'?[*] How do I appropriate the passion narrative with due proportion and without presumption?

Or, to put the matter more familiarly: by what means may I understand and experience Christ's wounds not just in juridical terms, as the providential means by which God chose to 'take away' sin, but as the living source of a remedy by which sin is cured and humanity's wounds, *my* wounds, are healed?

These are questions I will consider in the central chapter of this book. You will find it divided, like the *Rhythmica oratio*, into seven sections, each focusing on a particular

---

[*] Gal. 2.20.

part of the Saviour's crucified body, each introduced by the corresponding fragment of Arnulf of Leuven's poem.

A final chapter contextualizes the poem and considers its ramifications. This work, composed in solitude, poured forth from a monastic heart, turned into a fruitful source of cultural inspiration, even of song. I do not think it fanciful to recognize in this process a parable of how our wounds, healing, may turn to flourish, readying us to be of benefit and comfort to others.

Transformation

Ad pedes – To the Feet

Salve, mundi salutare:
Salve, salve, Jesu chare,
Cruci tuae me aptare
Vellem vere, tu scis quare
  Da mihi tui copiam.

Ac si praesens sis accedo,
Imo te praesentem credo.
O quam mundum hic te cerno!
Ecce tibi me prosterno:
  Sis facilis ad veniam.

Clavos pedum, plagas duras
Et tam graves impressuras
Circumplector cum affectu,
Tuo pavens in aspectu,
  Tuorum memor vulnerum.

Grates tantae charitati,
Nos agamus vulnerati.
O amator peccatorum,
Reparator confractorum:
  O dulcis pater pauperum!

Quidquid est in me confractum
Dissipatum, aut distractum,
Dulcis Jesu, totum sana,
Tu restaura, tu complana,
  Tam pio medicamine.

AD PEDES – TO THE FEET

Hail, salvation of the world:
Hail, beloved Jesus, hail.
Truly I wish to be fit for your cross.
You know why:
Admit me, Lord, into your presence.

I draw near as if you were present;
indeed I believe you are really here:
I perceive you, the most pure.
See, I prostrate myself before you:
Be liberal in granting pardon.

Deeply affected I embrace the nails
of your feet that leave such deep
impressions, such cruel sores.
Seeing you I shudder,
mindful of your wounds.

We, who are wounded, give thanks
for such great love,
O you who love sinners, restoring
those who have been broken,
sweet father of the poor.

Wholly cleanse, sweet Jesus,
restore and straighten
whatever in me is broken,
dissipated, distracted. Apply
your gracious medicine.

Te in tua cruce quaero,
Prout queo, corde mero;
Me sanabis hic, ut spero:
Sana me, et salvus ero,
  In tuo lavans sanguine,

Plagas tuas rubicundas,
Et fixuras tam profundas,
Cordi meo fac inscribi,
Ut configar totus tibi,
  Te modis amans omnibus.

Dulcis Jesu, pie Deus,
Ad te clamo licet reus:
Praebe mihi te benignum,
Ne repellas me indignum
  De tuis sanctis pedibus

Coram cruce procumbentem,
Hosque pedes complectentem,
Jesu bone, non me spernas,
Sed de cruce sancta cernas
  Compassionis gratia.

In hac cruce stans directe,
Vide me, o mi dilecte,
Ad te totum me converte:
Esto sanus, dic aperte,
  Dimitto tibi omnia.

AD PEDES – TO THE FEET

I look for you on your cross with
an integral heart as well as I can.
I hope you will heal me here.
Heal me and I shall be saved,
washed in your blood.

Cause your ruddy wounds,
the deep imprints of the nails,
to be inscribed on my heart,
that I may entirely be one with you,
loving you in every way.

Sweet Jesus, gracious God, even
though I who call to you am guilty,
show yourself benign in my regard,
drive me not away as one unworthy
from your sacred feet.

Headlong I lie before the cross,
I hold on to your feet:
good Jesus, spurn me not;
comprehend me with the grace
of compassion from your holy cross.

You, my beloved who stand upright
on this cross, look on me and
turn me wholly to yourself.
Speak openly to me: 'Be healed!
I forgive you everything.'

The first part of this poem, written almost 800 years ago, spells out a paradox to which Christians of all times are subject when, in faith, they consider Christ crucified. At one level we are disgusted by the cruelty of the scene. Our conscience stirs with resonances of the jeer launched at Alexamenos: is it not sick to fix our attention on such a monument to violence?

I heard a while ago of a young priest arriving in a parish newly assigned to him. He found there was no crucifix in the church. The parishioners explained: 'It is too depressing to look at.' It goes without saying that this point of view is misguided. It is well to ask *why* this is so.

It would seem that a hermeneutic shift essential to an outlook of faith has not taken place. If we avert our gaze from the cross on account of its unpleasantness, we are conscious of what the cross represents, but not of what it signifies. Let us consider the passage between these two stages of insight.

Abbot Arnulf sets out from a realistic appraisal, zooming in on details of the crucifixion scene. In this first section he directs our gaze towards the nails in Jesus's feet. They inflict harsh wounds. Metal just is not supposed to penetrate human flesh. There is a crying contrast between the suppleness of flesh, each tiniest fragment of which is alive, and the cruel, dead inflexibility of iron. There is outrage in the fact that God's handiwork created for movement in freedom, its feet like hind's feet,* should be arrested and disfigured by the craft of Tubal-cain.†

---

*2 Sam. 22.34.
†It was Tubal-cain, son of Lamech, a descendant of Cain, 'who made all kinds of bronze and iron tools', who was the first to manipulate nature in this way (Gen. 4.22).

AD PEDES – TO THE FEET

For the nails stand for human enterprise. In a short story written just after the First World War, the Norwegian novelist Johan Falkberget imagines how the nails for Jesus's crucifixion were forged in the Jerusalem smithy of the dissolute blacksmith Ela with iron his nameless slave had stolen under cover of night from the ancient structure of Solomon's Temple – iron that, according to legend, had been brought to the Holy Land from the northernmost reaches of the world, from a country whose mountains are covered in perpetual snow. For all his sweating and cursing, Ela was unable to make this iron red-hot, for 'all the world's frost and hardness was lodged in it'. It took all his strength to extract from it the three long nails required for the occupying power's capital punishment.[*]

The story is free invention. Yet it points by means of images to an essential truth. Face to face with the cross, we recognize our personal contribution to the nails that hold Christ captive to it.

Whatever our distance in space or time from Jesus's passion, we are complicit in its enactment. The nails stand for our iniquity: 'He was pierced for our faults,' we read in the prophet.[†] For their sake he 'must' suffer.[‡] The nails stand, too, for the frost and hardness of human hearts quite

---

[*] Johan Falkberget, *Naglerne eller Jernet fra Norden og andre fortællinger* (Kristiania: Aschehoug, 1921), p. 14.
[†] Isa. 53.5 according to the Jerusalem Bible often read in churches.
[‡] We considered, in the first chapter, this categorical 'must' in Mark. We find it in the other Gospels, too, e.g. Mt. 16.21, Lk. 9.22 and 17.25, Jn 3.14.

able, one moment, to shout 'Hosanna to the Son of David', then, the next: 'Crucify!'[*]

Christ's cross exemplifies absolute injustice, a violation of perennial, indeed of cosmic proportions. Of this we must not lose sight. Our perspective on the cross must be at least in part forensic.

At the same time, faith teaches us to see in the cross not just scandal and pain, but the love of which the cross is the sign. Love underlies Jesus's sacrifice, love 'to the end', still unexhausted.[†] In this fact there is sweetness. Not for nothing have Christians since earliest times perceived a type of the cross in the wood that Moses, at God's bidding, picked up and threw into the bitter waters of Marah, three days' travel up-country from the Red Sea just crossed. This wood made the bitter sweet.[‡]

Each year on Good Friday, the Church, a consummate pedagogue, leads us step by step through the liturgy, from disconsolate bitterness into sweet hope.

Good Friday's Commemoration of the Passion, a service unlike any other in the Church's year, is supposed to begin at three o'clock, the 'ninth hour' when Jesus cried out with a loud voice '*Eli, Eli, lema sabachtani?*' while darkness covered the land.[§] The service starts starkly. The congregation stands in silence. The priest enters the sanctuary wearing blood-red vestment. There, before the altar, he falls to the ground.

---

[*] Mt. 21.9, 27.22–3.
[†] Jn 13.1.
[‡] Exod. 15.22–5.
[§] Mt. 27.45f.

Prostration is the gesture of the suppliant and worshipper; it is also the gesture of one consumed with grief for whom the upward, vertical axis of life has lost its force of attraction, who is conscious only of being dust, lacking strength, perhaps even lacking will, to arise from dust.

This is, the Church tells us, the attitude we must assume if we wish to fathom the full reach of the mystery of Calvary. Rising, the priest prays on behalf of all:

Deus, qui peccati veteris hereditariam mortem, in qua posteritatis genus omne successerat, Christi Filii tui, Domini nostri, passione solvisti, da, ut conformes eidem facti, sicut imaginem terreni hominis naturae necessitate portavimus, ita imaginem caelestis, gratiae sanctificatione portemus.

God, all generations have succeeded each other in hereditary death resulting from ancient sin; you have dissolved it by the passion of Christ your Son, our Lord: grant that we, just as we have borne the image of earthly man by nature's necessity, may, conformed to him, bear the image of celestial man by the sanctification of grace.

I have tried to render the structure and thematic sequence of the Latin collect. The first image put before us is that of 'hereditary death'. This death is a feature of justice arising from 'ancient sin'. Since time's beginning death has monotonously swallowed up one generation after another in prospectless extinction. Our rightful inheritance culminates in non-being. Now, though, death, this previously all-overshadowing fixture of reality, has been 'dissolved'. The law it enforced has been rescinded. Death which, a moment ago, was life's only certainty is final no longer.

This is the effect of the passion of Christ, God's Son. It is not extrinsic to us. We are drawn into it and conformed to Christ through it, thus rendered fit to live differently. Whereas so far our purpose has been earthbound, subject to a necessary force of gravity, we are invited henceforth to look up, to envisage celestial, eternal, boundless life. We are no longer defined by need, but by grace that sanctifies. To be made holy is about more than being made good. Sanctification is transformation of our being. It does not cancel human nature, which is good in itself. But this nature is extended and fulfilled in so far as we become, by grace, participants in God's own nature.[*]

Allow me to remind you that this formula is read aloud by one who has just lain flat-out on the floor as if dead, just as we are about to rehearse the story of a death that, to those who witnessed it, appeared to spell the final eclipse of hope.[†]

The readings begin. We hear Isaiah proclaim with poignancy:

> He was bruised for our iniquities;
> upon him was the chastisement that made us whole,
>   and with his stripes we are healed.

---

[*] Gen. 1.31; 2 Pet. 1.4.
[†] Note the aorist tense, rendered in English as pluperfect, of the 'we had hoped' of the wanderers to Emmaus (Lk. 24.21), locating hope in an apparently unrecoverable past. The darkness that 'came over the whole land' (Lk. 23.44) when Jesus expired cast its shroud no less over human hearts.

AD PEDES — TO THE FEET

> All we like sheep have gone astray;
> we have turned every one to his own way;
> and the Lord has laid on him
> the iniquity of us all.[*]

The prophet admits that the exchange, *his* wounding for *our* healing, goes beyond the grasp of reason: 'Who has believed what we have heard?'[†]

The next reading, from Hebrews, stresses the priestly character of Christ's sacrifice.[‡] What is a priest if not one who makes of his life an oblation joined to the gifts he is ordained to offer on the altar that others may live?

The Passion according to St John then takes us in Jesus's footsteps to Calvary. We see blood and water flowing from his side, sealing the new, everlasting covenant. After Christ's words, 'It is accomplished,' the bowing of his head, the giving-up of his spirit, all present in the church, which seems to encompass the universe, fall to their knees. The Lord's body hangs lifeless, heavily, on the cross. At this point the cross is nothing but a gibbet of atrocious shame.

The liturgy, however, does not let us pause long in this state of paralysis. The reading of the passion is followed by the great intercessions peculiar to Good Friday. When we rise to pray, each of us stands enclosed, first, in his or her own grief. Our hearts then broaden. In solemn cadences we pray with an outreach that spreads like the circles on

---

[*] Isa. 53.5–6.
[†] Isa. 53.1.
[‡] Heb. 4.14–16, 5.7–9.

the surface of a calm forest lake into which you cast a pebble – or a piece of wood. We pray for the Church, for catechumens, for the unity of Christians, for the Jews, the chosen people God first made his own, for non-believers, for those in tribulation, that the Father Almighty

> may cleanse the world of all errors, banish disease, drive out hunger, unlock prisons, loosen fetters, granting to travellers safety, to pilgrims return, health to the sick, and salvation to the dying.[*]

There is something almost frantic in this widening embrace of the Church's prayer. No-one anywhere is excluded from the range of intercession. We, the downcast, stand erect. Our spirit rises. We ascertain that the river pouring forth from Jesus's side *has* cleansed the world and renewed it, the way the flood did in Noah's days. Sin is cancelled. Death is dissolved. Mercy materializes. No impurity remains outside its reach, provided we ourselves do not obstruct mercy.

After the intercessions, something grandiose happens. A large processional cross that stands for the one on which Christ died is carried through the church onto the sanctuary. It is covered in a violet veil. In a Scriptural frame of reference, a veil suggests the circumscription of glory.

In the first giving of the law on Mount Sinai, before the scandal of the golden calf, God asked Moses, on having the tabernacle built, to hang a veil before the inner sanctuary, the holy of holies where the mercy seat stood and the ark of

---

[*] From the tenth intercession for Good Friday, following the Roman Missal.

the covenant, sacraments of God's abiding presence.* The veil denoted the limit of sensual perception. It marked a reality of total otherness, *in* this world but not *of* it.

Later, when Moses ascended the mountain a second time, having chastised the people who, tired of waiting on the Lord, had sought more tangible satisfactions, he was led into a new degree of intimacy with God. The earthboundness of those he was called to govern required of him greater sublimity. Wrapt for 40 days in the vision of God, 'he neither ate bread nor drank water'. The requirements of his physical organism were apparently suspended. This exposure to God's presence left its mark visibly. When Moses returned to society, 'the skin of his face shone because he had been talking with God.' The radiance was more than people could endure; they were frightened to come near him. Moses therefore 'put a veil on his face', maintaining the shock of God's nearness and its impact within bearable bounds.†

The veil that covers the post-passion cross on Good Friday stands in symbolic continuity with these Old Testament veils. Think of Jesus's assurance that the 'lifting-up' of his suffering and death will somehow be full of light; that through these events God's glory, his perceptible presence, will manifest itself by way of an epiphany.‡ When Jesus 'cried out and breathed his last . . . the veil of the temple was rent

---

*Exod. 26.33.
†Exod. 34.29–35.
‡Cf. Jn 7.39, 12.23.

in two, from top to bottom'.* The mercy seat was displaced, reconfigured. The cross henceforth is the fount from which forgiveness flows, and reconciliation. God's glory has burst its bounds. It has flooded human experience, leaving no aspect of it untouched, not even that of felt dereliction.

Liturgically, this explosion is enacted through gradual unveiling. The priest removes the cross-veil in three stages: first from the right arm, then from the left, then from the cross's stem, showing forth Christ's wounded feet. At each stage he sings: 'Behold the wood of the cross, on which hung the salvation of the world.' The congregation answers: 'Come, let us adore!' The acclamation is made by way of a confession. Adoration is a human exercise whose only worthy object is God.

So transformation takes place before our eyes. The cross remains the cross, evil in itself. At the same time, we see it as the sign of God's definitive vanquishing of evil. The Crucified is not just 'Jesus of Nazareth', as Pilate the pragmatist wrote. He is our 'holy God, holy and strong, holy and immortal'. With these words, known to have been chanted in chorus by the Fathers of Chalcedon as a hymn to Christ, true man and true God, we profess our faith that the death-tree of human design has become a tree of life. Life attaches to it. There *is* glory there, but not of a kind that overwhelms and terrifies. Since God displays himself to us wounded, we dare to come before him with our wounds.

Thus the *Trisagion* resounds in its ancient modulations while a moving ritual takes place. One by one we come in

---

*Mt. 27.50f.

AD PEDES – TO THE FEET

slow procession before the cross to kiss Christ's crucified feet. The priest goes first, not on account of imagined privilege but because it is his sacramental duty to carry in advance, vicariously, all that which his faithful people carry. The rubrics prescribe that he should first remove his shoes. Like Moses before the burning bush, he approaches holy ground.[*] He is to be sensually conscious of his feet as he prostrates himself before those, immobile, of his Saviour. They were nailed to the cross so that his might move freely, directed towards a beatific goal. With the Psalmist he would shout: 'I have refrained my feet from every evil way.'[†] Before, he may have been 'like a bird rushing into a snare'.[‡] Restored fleetness of foot now keeps him secure: the fowler lays his traps henceforth in vain.[§]

To see the Good Friday congregation, full of well-known, well-loved faces but also of faces one has never seen before, come up to adore the cross, or rather, to adore him who, crucified, redeemed us, moves me viscerally every year. Each year I am conscious of this sight as a display of humanity owning the truth of itself, peacefully acknowledging the suffering by which no life is untouched yet holding its head high in trustful hope, in the certainty of being, remarkably, loved.

While this slow procession carries on, the choir, having finished the *Trisagion*, sings a hymn by Venantius

---

[*] Cf. Exod. 3.5.
[†] Psalm 119.101 in the KJV.
[‡] Prov. 7.23.
[§] Psalm 91.3.

Fortunatus, a wandering poet ordained to the priesthood late in life, then made bishop of Poitiers not long before his death in 609, a member of that contemplative movement which, after Chalcedon, developed a new language with which to speak of Christ's cross. It must be said: the words he uses are daring.

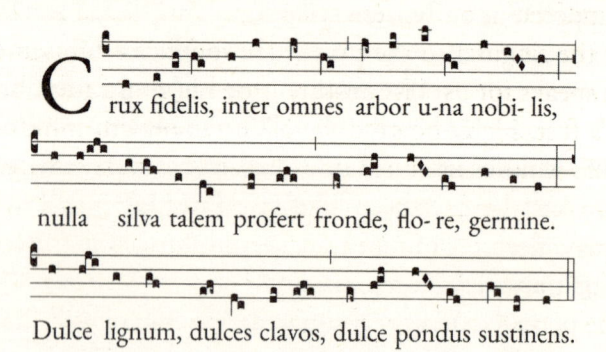

Crux fidelis, inter omnes arbor u-na nobi- lis,

nulla silva talem profert fronde, flo- re, germine.

Dulce lignum, dulces clavos, dulce pondus sustinens.

The cross is not here an object to be considered. It is addressed as if it were a person:

> Oh faithful cross, sole noble tree among all trees.
> No forest has brought forth your equal in foliage, flour or fruit.
> Sweet the wood, sweet the nails. Sweet the carried load.

The theme of sweetness explicit in the text recalls the miracle of Marah. It is brought out no less in the lilting tune composed in the first of the eight Gregorian modes. In the Middle Ages, people called the first mode 'grave', *gravis*, on account of its wide range and minor-key tonality. But there is exultation in it, too. To hear it, to sing it, in this singular

AD PEDES — TO THE FEET

setting is to gain a new perspective on the words: 'It is accomplished.' Death has revealed itself a source of life. The cross stands before us, now, not only as proof of heroic love, not only as a mark of judicial victory, but also as something loveable and dear. Like death, it has lost its sting.[*]

I have tried to trace the contours of a backdrop presupposed in our Cistercian poem. The poet moves easily from the singular to the plural. He speaks for himself even as he speaks for us. His posture is one of prostration before Jesus's feet. Here, he says, we all lie wounded, mindful of Christ's wounds in gratitude and awe. It is noteworthy that he invokes the Lord with the epithet 'sweet', *Dulcis Iesu*. We may discern in this choice of a word the full range of connotation we have looked at.

The perspective described in this opening section 'To the Feet' establishes the outlook of the text as a whole both as literature and as theology. This is Christology from below. The fourth-century Desert Father Evagrius is often quoted as having said that a theologian is a man who prays. His actual statement, in the sixty-first of his *Chapters on Prayer*, is a little more complex. He wrote: 'If you are a theologian, you will truly pray; and if you pray truly, you will be a theologian.'[†] Evagrius's truth criterion regards more than the content of reflection. At stake is attitude. It seems to me that Arnulf, prostrate before Christ's crucified feet, conscious of encountering there the self-outpouring, self-sacrificing charity of *God*, exemplifies the stance of one who

---

[*] 1 Cor. 15.55.
[†] Εἰ θεολόγος εἶ, προσεύξῃ ἀληθῶς· καὶ εἰ ἀληθῶς προσεύχῃ, θεολόγος ἔσῃ.

is a true Christian theologian. Were more theology written from this vantage point, one would be spared a great deal of nonsense.

To set out from consideration of Christ's feet establishes, in addition, a tone of intimate vulnerability. Some time ago I read a remarkable book, the *Confessions of a Chiropodist*. The writer reveals an interesting fact: all her patients (she insists this is a rule without exception) ask, when they first turn up, forgiveness for their feet – for the general state of them, their shape, their relative smallness or largeness.[*] Most of us, it seems, are ashamed of our feet. That explains, perhaps, why so many people are reluctant to take part in the foot-washing on Maundy Thursday. It sheds light, too, on what went on that night, long ago, in the Upper Room. When Jesus took the feet of the Twelve, one by one, into his hands it was to say: 'I know you as you are, I love you as you are.' It is an experience none of them was able to forget.

Prostrate before the Crucified's feet we see *him* as he is in his incarnate reality. The eternal Word humbled himself when he consented to be born an infant; when he, the principle of motion, was wrapped in tight swaddling clothes. But nowhere is his self-outpouring more evident than in his pierced, exposed, afflicted feet. There is intimate delicacy in Arnulf's twice repeated, comforting gesture of embracing them.

---

[*] Katja Oskamp, *Marzahn, mon amour*, trans. Jo Heinrich (London: Peirene, 2022). 'Confessions of a Chiropodist' is the subtitle to the original German edition.

AD PEDES – TO THE FEET

We constantly, sometimes recklessly, rehearse before the crucifix our wants, our needs, our frustrations. We cry for help. But are we aware that God, the all-compassionate, whose crucified state remains ineffably real and efficacious, as Pascal wrote, until the end of time, may also call out for our compassion?[*]

To be concrucified with Christ, in Paul's terms,[†] or to be 'fitted for his cross', to cite Arnulf of Leuven, is not about principles only. The process is not confined to our mind. It begins with our feet, with how we direct them, with whether we move when called to walk and have the guts to stand still when it is time to remain.

> Lord Jesus, may the sight of your wounded feet remind
> me of the promise and consequence of each step
> I make with mine. Amen.

---

[*] '*Jésus sera en agonie jusqu'à la fin du monde. Il ne faut pas dormir pendant ce temps-là*', *Pensée* 553 in the Brunschvicg edition.
[†] Gal. 2.20.

Ad genua – To the Knees

Salve, Jesu, rex sanctorum,
spes votiva peccatorum,
Crucis ligno tanquam reus
Pendens homo verus Deus,
　　Caducis nutans genibus.

O quam pauper! o quam nudus!
Qualis es in cruce ludus
Derisorum totus factus,
Sponte tamen, non coactus,
　　Attritus membris omnibus!

Sanguis tuus abundanter
Fusus, fluit incessanter,
Totus lotus in cruore,
Stas in maximo dolore,
　　Praecinctus vili tegmine.

O Majestas infinita!
O egestas inaudita!
Quis pro tanta charitate,
Quaerit te in veritate,
　　Dans sanguinem pro sanguine

Quid sum tibi responsurus,
Actu vilis, corde durus?
Quid rependam amatori,
Qui elegit pro me mori,
　　Ne dupla morte morerer?

AD GENUA — TO THE KNEES

Hail, Jesus, king of saints
and sinners' votive hope, hanging
as if guilty on the wood of the cross,
you, the man who in truth are God,
your sunken knees wavering.

How derelict you are, how naked!
On the cross you have wholly
been made into a scoffers' plaything.
But it is freely, not under constraint
that you are spent in all your members.

Abundantly your poured-out blood
flows without ceasing.
Wholly washed in blood,
You stand in an extremity of pain,
girded with a vile garment.

O infinite majesty!
O unheard-of want!
Who for such charity's sake
will seek you in truth,
giving his blood for yours?

What can I say to you, I who am
vile in action, hard of heart?
How can I repay the lover
who chose to die for me lest
I suffer a twofold death?

Amor tuus amor fortis,
Quem non vincunt jura mortis:
O quam pia me sub cura,
Tua foves in pressura,
   Ne morsu mortis vulnerer!

Ecce tuo prae amore,
Te complector cum rubore:
Me coapta diligenter,
Tu scis causam evidenter,
   Sed suffer et dissimula.

Hoc quod ago non te gravet,
Sed me sanet et me lavet
Inquinatum et aegrotum,
Sanguis fluens hic per totum,
   Ut non supersit macula.

In hac cruce te cruentum,
Te contemptum et distentum,
Ut requiram, me impelle,
Et hoc imple meum velle,
   Facturus quod desidero.

Ut te quaeram mente pura,
Sit haec mea prima cura.
Non est labor, nec gravabor
Sed sanabor et mundabor,
   Cum te complexus fuero.

AD GENUA — TO THE KNEES

Your love is a strong love
unvanquished by death's claims.
With what faithful care you nurse me
in the midst of affliction so that
death will not bite and wound me.

See, for the sake of your love
I embrace you, blushing for shame.
Restore me with care: you know all too well
the case to be made against me,
but bear it and conceal it.

May my action not weigh you down
but may your flowing blood
heal and cleanse me,
the impure and ailing, all over
so that not a single stain remains.

Impel me to look for you
bloody, despised, distended
here on this cross;
grant my wish
and do what I desire:

Let my first and foremost care
be to seek you with a pure mind.
To do so is not heavy or laborious;
no, when I embrace you
I shall be healed and purified.

I can place with precision my awakening to the religious significance of kneeling. I was nine, on holiday with my family on the north Adriatic coast in the country then still known as Yugoslavia. It was my first real trip abroad.

One day, on an excursion to Croatian Dubrovnik or Bosnian Mostar, I cannot remember which, we stopped in a church. We did so to withdraw for a while from the sun, which was fierce. Ours was not, on the whole, a church-going family. Such exposure as I had had to church life came from our local Lutheran parish. With the rest of the village we went there on Christmas Eve. The church looks now just as it did then: a spacious interior with white walls, a prominent pulpit, greyish-green pews, a house of God made for proclamation and listening, sitting and standing.

Footling about in this foreign ambiance, curiously dark, I decided to try and sit in one of the benches. I could not work out how to go about it. The people we had met out and about looked like us; but their furniture was funny. It invited a posture unknown to me, at once impractical and uncomfortable. The seats sloped. A raised foundation made it hard to sit properly, the way I had learnt to sit in church, with my knees at a tidy angle of 90 degrees.

I asked my parents what the purpose was of this design. They explained that it was made for kneeling. I remember I laughed. Not mockingly: there was nothing ridiculous about what I had been told. I laughed the way children do when they are faced with a kind of behaviour that is new and astonishing to them. The discovery of a public building organized in view of collective kneeling was a riddle. What would induce people to assume such an attitude? Why would they want to assume it? The sight of the kneelers remained among my most exotic impressions of the trip, one of those I told my friends about on coming home.

When you think about it, kneeling is counterintuitive. The human being is oriented upwards. Each of us, as children, passed from the supine to the upright state through an apprenticeship of unsteady intermediary poses. It is wonderful to see a child rise unsupported for the first time, standing up for itself. The Fathers saw in human verticality an indication of our calling: to keep our feet on the ground while we direct our body heavenwards even as we are called to lift up our hearts.

There is dignity in standing: not for nothing do we call a person of principle, an honourable woman or man, 'upstanding'. There is also joy. As a doctoral student, subject to back pain, I took lessons in the Alexander Technique, a pedagogy aimed at unlearning patterns of acquired physical misuse, to let our bodies function optimally, according to their natural structure. One day, practising correct standing, I heard my teacher say: 'Enjoy being tall!' I think that too made me laugh. I had never thought of standing as being intrinsically enjoyable. But it is. I think of that counsel to this day when I consciously correct myself out of a potato-sack slouch, straighten up and feel my whole organism breathe an exultant sigh of relief.

Of course, an effort to appear tall can be a way of imposing oneself on others. All depends on intention. Romano Guardini has written:

> When a man feels proud of himself, he stands erect, draws himself to his full height, throws back his head and shoulders and says with every part of his body, I am bigger and more important than you. But when he is humble he feels his littleness, and lowers his head and shrinks into himself. He abases himself. And the greater the presence in which he stands, the more deeply he abases himself; the smaller he becomes in his own eyes.

Guardini presents the posture of kneeling as an antidote to illusory presumption. We rightly fall to our knees faced with a transcendent reality worthy of homage. There is only one such: God. Once we awaken to the reality of who God is, and of who we, creatures of dust, are before God, kneeling becomes natural, almost necessary:

> One has no need to be told that God's presence is not the place in which to stand on one's dignity. To appear less presumptuous, to be as little and low as we feel, we sink to our knees and thus sacrifice half our height; and to satisfy our hearts still further we bow down our heads, and our diminished stature speaks to God and says, 'Thou art the great God; I am nothing.'

To kneel before God in this way amounts to a kinaesthetic confession. We bend our knee before him as an act of love. We do so with care, beautifully. A genuflexion should have something of the elegance of a curtsy. 'To kneel, in the soul's intention,' says Guardini, 'is to bow down before God in deepest reverence . . . It is an act of humility, an act of truth, and every time you kneel it will do your soul good.'[*]

To be noble and enobling, the act of kneeling must be free. To bring others to their knees despite themselves, constraining them to sham reverence, is cruel, a form of humiliation. Totalitarian systems everywhere have practised, and still practise, this method. We may think of images that have impressed themselves on global consciousness: of kneeling counter-revolutionaries lined up for public shaming during Chairman Mao's purges in China; of Viennese Jews forced out to clean the city's pavements on their knees after the *Anschluss*; or that of manacled, masked men in orange jumpsuits kneeling in detention at Guantánamo Bay.[†] The sight of such scenes has made kneeling abhorrent to many, a symbol of oppression. Some may have decided: 'I shall kneel to no-one.' Such a decision, readily comprehensible, may, though, stunt a deeply human impetus and instinct.

For do we not yearn, deep down, for a just cause to kneel? Wolfgang Büscher, a perspicacious chronicler of

---

[*] *Sacred Signs*, trans. Grace Branham (St Louis: Pio Decimo Press, 1956), pp. 19–20.

[†] The photograph of this scene that caused international sensation was taken by a United States Navy photographer and, this is noteworthy, *intentionally* released by the US Defense Department. See Carol Rosenberg's piece, '20 Years Later, the Story Behind the Guantánamo Photo That Won't Go Away', in the *New York Times* of 10 January 2022.

travel, has spoken of his long search, high and low, 'for a reason to kneel and for a place upon this earth in which to bend my knee':

> We don't do it any more, and don't want to, not before anyone . . . For me it was different. I was conscious sometimes of a deep inner need to kneel. I do not consider this humiliating in any way. To be humble and humiliated are two different things. In so far as I am humble this is a sense that arises within me; humiliation, by contrast, is forced upon me from outside to cast me down and keep me down.

Büscher says that the act of kneeling may have a chivalrous aspect. I can be a self-respecting and in the best sense proud human being yet acknowledge that something is greater than I, that this something deserves my reverence, and that its performance, even as I bow down, elevates me. Büscher's physical need to kneel, carried for years as an emptiness of non-fulfilment, played into his Christian conversion. The liturgy let the emptiness be filled, most emblematically in the moment before Holy Communion when, in the Catholic Mass, the communicant kneels, beats his breast and says, 'Lord, I am not worthy to receive you, but only say the word, and I shall be healed.' Büscher confides that 'years had to pass before I could speak this phrase without deep inner emotion. This phrase, and the accompanying action, give form to the realization that we are not complete in ourselves.' It seems to him, as it seems to me, that there is in all of us a soul-space in which we have knowledge of these things, but the key to that space is mostly lost.*

Perhaps it is only on our knees that we can find it. Sometimes we must take the risk of kneeling *first*, like Charles de Foucauld famously did on 30 October 1886. Having returned eight months earlier from military service in Morocco, he, whose life was marked by dissipation, had been stirred by the sight of Muslims at prayer, provoked to revisit the tenets of the faith in which he had been raised. It was to discuss these that he made his way that morning, a declared agnostic, to the confessional of Father Huvelin in the Paris church of St-Augustin. The priest was graced with an exceptional knowledge of souls. He had a well-attested gift of discernment. He sensed that what this young man truly sought was not explanations but an encounter with truth, and that he had to be disposed to receive it. Huvelin told him: 'Kneel and make your confession.' Foucauld declined at first, then did, remarkably, as he was told. He found thereby that a long and arduous struggle was over. Looking back, he wrote: 'At once I believed that there was a God; I understood that I could not do anything other than live only for him.'†

The second section of Arnulf's poem is entitled *Ad genua*, 'To the Knees'. It is ostensibly a reflection on the knees of

---

*For clarity's sake I have slightly condensed Büscher's oral testimony, given as part of an initiative launched by the Catholic Academy of Berlin in 2016. The video from which I cite can be found online at www.alpha-omega-letters.de under the heading 'Niederknien'.
†Jean-François Six, *Vie de Charles de Foucauld* (Paris: Seuil, 1962), pp. 31f.

Christ crucified, resistanceless in weakness. But it is just as much about the praying subject's knees. Having begun his prayer lying prostrate, he has now raised his upper body. A kneeling position is the only one in which he can realistically embrace the Saviour's knees.

The starkness of the scene is evoked with its blood, gore and 'extremity of pain'. The paradox of powerless omnipotence is stressed. In faith we confess the crucified body as majesty divine, but the connection is not self-evident.

This fact is acknowledged in the penultimate stanza, in the prayer: 'Impel me to look for you/bloody, despised, distended/here on this cross.' To look on the cross is not necessarily to see its mystery unfold; we must look *for* it by conscious effort, piercing again and again familiarity's blinding fog. Purity of mind is called for. It presupposes a patiently nurtured ecology of soul.

Another needed quality of perception can be traced in the *rubor* of the seventh stanza. 'Rubor' is no intellective faculty. It means 'redness' and normally refers to blushing. Blood rises to our cheeks in the realization that we have an instrumental share in the cross's necessity not just on account of our being, in principle and somewhat abstrusely, partakers 'in Adam',[*] but by virtue of particular sins we have committed, which call out to be borne and repaired.

With Arnulf we pray: 'May my action not weigh you down.' But we know that it does; that there *is* a deathly heaviness in our betrayals; and that Christ does carry them, singly and in their totality.

---

[*] 1 Cor. 15.22.

AD GENUA – TO THE KNEES

To kneel in this awareness is to show humility. Kneeling also represents, for one whose starting point was unseeing alignment to the ground, a rising to responsibility in truth. To look straight at Christ's 'wavering knees' unable by the cross's cunning contraption to support even his body weight, which pulls on his hands, and to know, 'I am in this', is to reconsider everything.

Who would not, faced with this sight, make earnest resolutions for the amendment of one's life? Prayer for healing and purification is made in view of a purpose: to somehow repay such total love and to do so by self-outpouring, certain that this is the path that leads to life, the antithesis of that 'twofold' death which results from a narrow-minded outlook on life that seeks only self-preservation: 'For anyone who keeps his life for himself shall lose it.'[*]

Kneeling is a characteristically biblical posture, not much to the fore in other civilizations. Historians of antiquity despised it as unworthy of free men. Aristotle thought it barbarous.[†] In Scripture it takes time for kneeling to emerge as a dignified, beautiful attitude. In fact, the first time kneeling is mentioned in the Bible, it does not refer to human beings at all, but to the ten camels Abraham's manservant brought with him from Canaan to Mesopotamia on his mission to find a wife for Isaac, his master's son.

---

[*] Mt. 16.25.
[†] For a helpful contextualization of kneeling, see the section on 'Kneeling/Prostration' in Joseph Ratzinger's *The Spirit of the Liturgy*, trans. John Saward (San Francisco: Ignatius Press, 2000).

Arrived in Aram-naharaim 'he made his camels kneel down by the well of water; it was towards evening, the time when women go out to draw water.'* The kneeling camels had a providential role to play. Rebekah's prompt offer to give them to drink showed her forth as the bride the Lord had chosen. Still, this is hardly a sublime precedent.

The next instance of kneeling is inglorious, too. It occurs towards the end of Genesis, when Joseph, Rebekah's grandson, is raised up after incarceration in Egypt, a result of Potiphar's wife's shady dealings. Not only has he been released from prison; he has become a pharaonic high official. Pharaoh, on giving Joseph a signet ring and precious clothes, let him 'ride in the chariot of his second-in-command; and they cried out in front of him: Bow the knee!'† It is an incident that rather proves Aristotle's point.

Only with the post-Exodus establishment of Israel's cult does kneeling emerge as a distinct devotional gesture. In the wonderful chapter of the First Book of Kings that recounts the consecration of the temple in Jerusalem, Solomon, having first 'stood before the altar of the Lord in the presence of all the assembly of Israel', pronounces a lengthy prayer that explicates the function of this house of sacrifice and intercession, asking that the eyes of God 'may be open night and day towards this house, the place of which you said, "My name shall be there", that you may heed the prayers that your servant prays towards this place'. There repentant sinners may seek pardon, the grieving consolation, foreigners

---

*Gen. 24.11.
†Gen. 41.43.

AD GENUA – TO THE KNEES

justice; there God's mercy will assuredly flow; there the legacy of Moses will live. We do not know at what point of the oration Solomon fell to his knees, but are told that when he had finished, 'he arose from facing the altar of the Lord, where he had knelt with hands outstretched towards heaven; he stood and blessed all the assembly.'*

The hallowing of a stable dispensation of grace, a mark of divine condescension and election, called for a visible acknowledgement of favour on the part of the people's representative. In Solomon all Israel kneels. A paradigm is fixed that will henceforth define right worship, canonized in a Psalm of praise: 'Come, let us worship and bow down, let us kneel before the Lord, our Maker! For he is our God, and we are the people of his pasture, and the sheep of his hand.'†

Such gracious kneeling in response to grace is contrasted with kneeling before an unworthy object. The Lord's announcement to Elijah that he will cut off from the land all who have bent their knees to Baal is kept alive in Israel's remembrance, cited by St Paul in his letter to the Romans as an indication of how a remnant is formed, apt to receive and communicate grace.‡

In the New Testament, suppliants kneel before Jesus. The earliest of these, in the first chapter of Mark, is interesting.

---

*1 Kgs 8.22, 29, 54f.
†Psalm 95.6f. Psalm 95 is the Psalm St Benedict set as the Invitatory, which formally introduces each new day's round of worship at the nocturnal office of Vigils.
‡1 Kgs 19.18; Rom. 11.4.

In modern editions we read of a leper who came up to Christ in Galilee 'begging him and kneeling', saying, 'If you choose you can make me clean.'[*] The specification 'and kneeling' is lacking from several early Gospel manuscripts. It may represent a separate tradition; it may be an amendment added not to falsify, but to bring out the dynamic of the scene read in the light of the Church's mature understanding of who Jesus is.

Given the stature of kneeling in biblical thought, the leper's action would bear witness to Jesus's identity, a confession of his lordship. In verse one of chapter one of Mark, 'The beginning of the good news of Jesus Christ, the Son of God', the phrase 'Son of God' is likewise lacking in some early witnesses: many of those that have it also have the addition about the leper's kneeling later. This fact alerts us to the Christological significance of the gesture. It sheds light on the sentiments of Arnulf's poem, too. We kneel before the cross not just on account of exhaustion or to reverence human pain. Our kneeling enacts recognition of who is suspended before us: a man who in truth is God, his 'sunken knees wavering'.

The passion narratives present Jesus on his knees in the garden of Gethsemane. The scene as set by Luke is tragic:

> And he came out, and went, as was his custom, to the Mount of Olives; and the disciples followed him. And when he came to the place he said to them, 'Pray that you may not enter into temptation.' And he withdrew from them

---

[*] Mk 1.40. For further such instances, cf. Mk 10.17, Mt. 17.14.

AD GENUA – TO THE KNEES

about a stone's throw, and knelt down and prayed, 'Father, if thou art willing, remove this cup from me; nevertheless not my will, but thine, be done.' And when he rose from prayer, he came to the disciples and found them sleeping for sorrow, and he said to them, 'Why do you sleep? Rise and pray that you may not enter into temptation.'[*]

The kneeling of God's Son is a sign of adoration of the Father's will, which is a loving will for all to be saved,[†] yet nonetheless an ordinance that spells, in the immediate term, a sacrifice so full it seems unbearable. The prayer Jesus makes on his knees for the impending cup to pass gives us a glimpse of his inner life, of the battle that even an immaculate humanity must fight to answer the exigence of divinity defined by self-outpouring. The sight of God himself exposed to temptation inspires awe. Jesus's example in the garden spurs us on to assume our own battles in his name forthrightly, fortified by prayer, ready, like him, to rise up from prayer freely to *embrace* whatever trial is in store.

The world cannot know what this kind of struggle amounts to. There is a haunting depiction of this scene in Pasolini's film *The Gospel of St Matthew* from 1964. Pasolini was far removed from the sensibility of conventional piety; he was well versed in the registers of human passion. That may be why he was able to leave us such a compelling account of the agony the Son of God sustained on his knees.

---

[*] Lk. 22.39–46.
[†] 1 Tim. 2.4.

Having shown us how Jesus exhorted his disciples, 'Watch with me', only to see them fall uneasily asleep; having shown him fall to the ground three times, sweat pouring from his brow; showing him kneeling in prayer, 'Father, if it is possible!', Pasolini broadens his lens to take in the landscape in which this drama with eternal consequence plays out. In the background, across the Kidron Valley, Jerusalem lazily awakens at dawn. Fires are lit; we hear the gentle sounds of a world emerging from sleep. Suddenly a fellow on the other side – the other side of the brook but no less on the other side of reality – starts whistling to himself, out on his way to fetch wood, perhaps, or to care for his beasts.

God is sweating blood. The world's salvation is played out. And you, whoever you are, go about whistling? The contrast is immense, but recognizable. We have all experienced something of the kind: when someone we love has died, when we have received a serious diagnosis, when we are betrayed in friendship, when we have done something despicable: time seems to stand still. All our attention, all our powers of soul, are absorbed by this one, all-embracing reality; yet the world carries on regardless. We cannot fathom it. Are people around us then deaf and blind? Grief and rage can arise in us at such times as from an erupting volcano.

To see the knees on which Christ knelt in adoration fixed in quivering exhaustion, powerless to sustain, powerless to bend, is to confront in physiological detail the outrage humanity wrought on Love incarnate, which nonetheless remains determined and effective. How do I position myself before it here and now with my drooping hands and weak knees?* Will I add to Love's burden, or alleviate it?

Lord Jesus, let me never bend my knees to anything unworthy of worship, sooner smite my knees if you must. Let your sacred passion make me strong to persist in prayer and to find in my perseverance, joined with yours, peace.

---

*Cf. Heb. 12.12.

Ad manus – To the Hands

Salve, Jesu, pastor bone,
Fatigatus in agone,
Qui per lignum es distractus,
Et ad lignum es compactus,
    Expansis sanctis manibus.

Manus sanctae, vos avete,
Rosis novis adimplete,
Hos ad ramos dure junctae,
Et crudeli ferro punctae
    Tot guttis decurrentibus

Ecce fluit circumquaque
Manu tua de utraque,
Sanguis tuus copiose,
Rubicundus instar rosae,
    Magnae salutis pretium.

Manus clavis perforatas,
Et cruore purpuratas,
Corde primo prae amore,
Sitibundo bibens ore,
    Cruoris stillicidium.

O quam large te exponis
Promptus malis atque bonis!
Trahis pigros, pios vocas,
Et in tuis ulnis locas,
    Paratus gratis omnibus.

AD MANUS – TO THE HANDS

Hail Jesus, good shepherd,
exhausted in battle,
drawn out on wood,
fastened to the wood,
your sacred hands extended.

I salute you, sacred hands,
harshly joined to these branches,
pierced by cruel iron. From you
plentiful drops drip down.
Be filled with freshly sprung roses!

See, round about,
from both your hands,
your rose-red blood
flows copiously as the price
of a great salvation.

For love my heart presses
your hands that are punctured by nails,
purpled with blood.
With my mouth, meanwhile, I thirstily
drink drops of your blood that was shed.

You show yourself broad,
ready to receive both good and bad;
attracting the indolent, calling the devout,
holding them in your embrace,
freely open to all.

Ecce tibi me praesento,
Vulnerato et cruento:
Semper aegris misereris;
De me ergo ne graveris
    Qui praesto es amantibus,

In hac cruce sic intensus,
In te meos trahe sensus,
Meum posse, velle, scire,
Cruci tuae fac servire,
    Me tuis apta brachiis.

In tam lata charitate
Trahe me in veritate,
Propter crucem tuam almam,
Trahe me ad crucis palmam,
    Dans finem meis vitiis.

Manus sanctae, vos amplector,
Et gemendo condelector;
Grates ago plagis tantis,
Clavis duris, guttis sanctis,
    Dans lacrymas cum osculis.

In cruore tuo lotum,
Me commendo tibi totum:
Tuae sanctae manus istae
Me defendant, Jesu Christe,
    Extremis in periculis.

AD MANUS — TO THE HANDS

See, I present myself before you
as you are: wounded and bleeding.
You unfailingly have pity on the sick.
Do not count me a dead weight, you,
the protector of those who do love.

Strained in this way on the cross,
draw my senses towards you:
let my ability, my knowledge, my will
serve the cause of your cross;
conform me to your outstretched arms.

Draw me in truth,
in your charity drawn-out in this way,
for the sake of your nurturing cross;
draw me to the cross's victory,
and put an end to my vices.

Sacred hands, I embrace you,
I find in you, with sighs, my delight;
I give thanks for your deep wounds,
for the hard nails and sacred blood-drops;
I kiss you with tears.

Washed in your blood,
I commend myself wholly to you;
Jesus Christ, may your sacred hands
defend me
in the perils of my last agony.

In the Hebrew Bible, the 'hand' of the Lord stands for agency. This can be the case in a purely formal way. The expression 'by the hand of' can sustain the general sense 'by means of'. There is not necessarily an anthropomorphic notion of handling at work. We have to do with a metaphor, a phenomenon of language.

Linguistic phenomena, however, are rarely arbitrary.

The fact that Israel conceived of God as touching created reality to form it by his 'hand' shows biblical faith in God's nearness. Israel's God is no unmoved mover. He keeps his hand in the development and flourishing of what he has made. His hand manifests his providence, which, as a splendid collect says, never fails.[*]

From the outset, a special relationship obtains between God's hand and the human species. At the beginning of Genesis, the universe comes into being in response to a series of majestic proclamations. The process of gradual distinction between light and darkness, the waters above and the waters below, sea and dry land is accomplished by divine command: 'God said . . . and it was so.' Only when the making of man is recounted are we told that 'the Lord God formed man from dust of the ground, and breathed into his nostrils the breath of life.'[†]

The hand of God is not mentioned explicitly, but is taken for granted. The Hebrew verb employed to render

---

[*] 'Deus, cuius providentia in sui dispositione non fallitur, te supplices exoramus, ut noxia cuncta submoveas, et omnia nobis profutura concedas', set for Week 9 of Ordinary Time.
[†] Gen. 2.7.

AD MANUS – TO THE HANDS

the idea of forming, *vayyitzer*, derives from a root, *yatzar*, typically used to speak of a potter moulding his clay, the archetype of manufacture. The verb is later used with reference to animals, too: 'So out of the ground the Lord God formed every animal of the field and every bird of the air',[*] though with a significant distinction. When it refers to the creation of man, the verb is spelt with a double *yod* (the first consonant in the three-letter root); where the creation of animals is concerned, there is one *yod* only. The Rabbis interpret this variant spelling as follows: 'Man alone, they declare, is endowed with both a *Yetzer tob* (a good inclination) and a *Yetzer ra* (an evil inclination); whereas animals have no moral discrimination or moral conflict. Another explanation is: man alone is a citizen of two worlds; he is both of earth and of heaven.'[†] Having formed him, God breathed into him a soul, an action unparalleled in the creation of beasts. To this inspiration man owes his unique, sublime potential to become 'like' God.[‡]

When the 'hand' of God appears in biblical history, it is often in connection with moral instruction, to assist the human inclination for good in such a way that it gains the upper hand in battle against our inclination for evil. Sometimes, too, God's 'hand' intervenes to save man from

---

[*] Gen. 2.19.
[†] I am citing a footnote from *The Pentateuch and Haftorahs: Hebrew Text with English Translation and Commentary* ed. J. H. Hertz (London: Soncino Press, 2001), p. 7.
[‡] Gen. 1.26; 2.7.

himself, when he has lost direction, is stuck or has got himself into intractable trouble.

The most emblematic of such scenarios is the exodus from Egypt. Before we look into it, we need to consider the symbolic charge of Egypt in Scripture, more variegated than we might at first think.

Egypt was at the outset a sanctuary for Israel. Had the sons of Jacob not been able to settle there, had Joseph not become an Egyptian official, the tribes would have perished for hunger in a cruel famine.[*] Egypt offered Israel more than just grain; they found goodness there as well. There is a thought-provoking account of Egyptian righteousness already in the epic of Abram. He, too, went down to Egypt to seek sustenance in times of famine, tracing the route his descendants would follow generations later.

On entering the land, he thought up a puzzling ruse that blemishes his character, revealing that even this patriarch of patriarchs was subject to the twofold *yetzer* and must *learn* to act rightly. For there are no two ways about it: coming into Egypt, Abram lied. He said to Sarai, his wife,

> I know that you are a woman beautiful to behold; and when the Egyptians see you, they will say, 'This is his wife'; then they will kill me, but they will let you live. Say you are my sister, that it may go well with me because of you, and that my life may be spared on your account.[†]

---

[*] Gen. 42.1f.
[†] Gen. 12.11f.

AD MANUS – TO THE HANDS

This she did. What Abram had predicted took place. Sarai 'was taken into Pharaoh's house' while Abram was left in peace to tend his flock.[*]

Poor Pharaoh suffered afflictions. These he found to be a scourge sent from above on account of malfeasance. When he learned that Sarai had become part of his household on false pretences, he saw the connection. His response was honourable. Instead of just getting rid of Abram, a resident alien few would miss, and keeping his lovely wife for himself, the way David later acted with regard to Uriah,[†] Pharaoh reproached Abram and, peeved to have been snared into injustice, said, 'What is this you have done to me? Why did you not tell me she was your wife?' He let Sarai go. Abram was allowed to make his way back to the promised land and to take his goods with him, possessions 'very great'. There is no hint of any sanction.[‡]

Keeping these incidents in mind we shall eschew a too facile reading of the exodus and its meaning in our lives. We shall remember that what 'Egypt' represents in the Bible is not all bad. The humanity of Pharaoh's daughter enabled the survival of Moses, who gloried in the title 'friend of God'.[§] As a youth he was 'educated in all the wisdom of the Egyptians'. It equipped him for his providential task.[¶] Before the Israelites set out on their journey, they found

---

[*] Gen. 12.15f.
[†] 2 Sam.11.
[‡] Gen. 12.18–20, 13.6.
[§] Exod. 2.5–10, 33.7–11.
[¶] Acts 7.22.

'favour in the sight of the Egyptians' and were given much Egyptian silver, gold and clothing, resources that stood them in good stead in the wilderness.[*] Some of the gold was used for making the golden calf, but some for making sacred vessels, furnishing the sacristy of Israel's cult. Egypt had been home enough to Israel for some to feel homesick for it, rather like Lot's wife looked back on Sodom with nostalgia.[†]

By the time Moses was born, Israelites and Egyptians lived in conflict on account of anxieties that point forward towards modern geopolitics. The Israelites, arrived in Egypt as refugees on humanitarian grounds to become a useful workforce, were seen as a threat when they grew in numbers and self-confidence. The prospect of demographic imbalance provoked the measures imposed when 'a new king arose over Egypt, who did not know Joseph', that is, who did not remember how God had kept his hand over Jacob's sons and how Joseph had let Egypt thrive in hard times.

> He said to his people: 'Look, the Israelite people are more numerous and more powerful than we. Come, let us deal shrewdly with them, or they will increase and, in the event of war, join our enemies and fight against us and escape from the land.'[‡]

---

[*] Exod. 12.35f.
[†] Num. 11.5; Gen. 19.26.
[‡] Exod. 1.8f.

AD MANUS – TO THE HANDS

This new Pharaoh, probably Rameses II, had no use for notions of providence in the establishment of policy. What he believed in was pragmatic shrewdness enforced through violent means by state agencies.

We see the outline of a confrontation in idealistic terms between two world views. In the Mosaic period, Egypt represents a despotic system of nationalist ambition that endeavours to maintain a *status quo* of autonomous dominance. Israel, meanwhile, represents theocracy fluid in movement, tribal in origin but universal in scope, able to integrate forthwith, still on the Egyptian side of the Red Sea, a multitude of mixed ethnic and cultural extraction,[*] ready to take on board and realize the prophecy given to Abram before he set out from Haran: 'in you all the families of the earth shall be blessed.'[†]

These rival tendencies are spoken of in Scripture as the 'hand' of Pharaoh versus the 'hand' of the Lord. Having called Moses from within the burning bush to lead Israel home, God made clear the stakes of the task in hand well before negotiations with Pharaoh had begun: 'I know that the king of Egypt will not let you go unless compelled by a mighty hand. So I will stretch out my hand and strike Egypt.'[‡] The Lord's hand accompanies Israel faithfully from then on, not only in the plagues that prepare the people's departure from Egyptian soil. At the Red Sea Moses's

---

[*] Exod. 12.38.
[†] Gen. 12.3.
[‡] Exod. 3.19f.

'outstretched hands' enact the saving work of 'the right hand' of the Lord, saving Israel from 'the hand of Pharaoh'.[*]

Later, on Sinai, God hands to Moses tablets of stone that his divine hand had inscribed, containing the commandments.[†] When the people face the frontier of the land, Moses asks them to look back, saying: 'the Lord your God bore you, as a man bears his son, in all the way that you went until you came to this place.'[‡] The Exodus metaphor by which God's saving power is portrayed as a predator's pinions ('I bore you on eagles' wings'[§]) is repurposed as a loving father's carrying hands.

The recalcitrants of Israel were kept from homecoming because 'the Lord's own hand was against them, to root them out from the camp, until all had perished.'[¶] Having made their hearts bitter and their hands ineffective through murmuring, they were unfit for beatitude. As for those blessed to cross the Jordan, they are told that even this longed-for haven points beyond itself to a still more glorious reality. At the end of the day, 'the eternal God is your dwelling place, and underneath are the everlasting arms.'[**] Moses spoke these words before he breathed his last at the foot of Mount Nebo in the land of Moab. There he

---

[*] Exod. 14.16, 15.6, 18.10.
[†] Exod. 24.12, 31.18.
[‡] Deut. 1.31.
[§] Exod. 19.4.
[¶] Deut. 2.15.
[**] Deut. 33.27.

AD MANUS – TO THE HANDS

was buried, some say, by God's own hands in a grave made ready for him at creation.*

As a figure of speech 'the Lord's hand' is refined throughout the Pentateuch. It left its mark on the rest of the Bible and on the consciousness of believers. God's hands are conceived of as perpetually forming and guiding Israel, chastising or caressing as needed, leading the people to accomplish the purpose for which it was called into being. Jeremiah, preaching at a time when the 'hand' of Egypt again interfered with Israel's destiny, suggestively brings together different strands of significance in one of the tableaux he uses as didactic devices:

> The word that came to Jeremiah from the Lord: 'Arise, and go down to the house of the potter [*yotzer*], and there I will let you hear my words.' So I went down to the potter's house, and there he was working at his wheel. And the vessel he was making of clay was spoiled in the potter's hand, and he reworked it into another vessel, as it seemed good to the potter to do. Then the word of the Lord came to me: 'O house of Israel, can I not do with you as this potter has done? says the Lord. Behold, like the clay in the potter's hand, so are you in my hand, O house of Israel.'†

---

*Deut. 34.6. The tradition regarding Moses's burial is cited in Hertz's *Pentateuch and Haftorahs* on p. 916, referencing the Ethics of the Father, V.6.
†Jer. 18.1–6.

To be an Israelite, a child of God, is to stay within God's shaping hands as he, the all-knowing *Yotzer*, directs our twofold *yetzer* according to a purpose of beauty.

When we contemplate the crucifix, it is outrageous to see the Lord's hands paralysed and disfigured, pierced by nails made according to the measures of Roman penal practice, knocked through flesh, bones and sinews by a hammer held in a hand that might as well, symbolically speaking, count as Pharaoh's.

> Hail Jesus, good shepherd,
> exhausted in battle,
> drawn out on wood,
> fastened to the wood,
> your sacred hands extended.

The shepherd's hands, which we count upon to hold a staff and crook, to prepare a joyful banquet, to anoint his flock, one by one, with sanctifying oil, are motionless now, and limp.[*] They seem inactive; but no, they are raised still, extended like Moses's were, first over the Red Sea, then over Israel fighting Amalek, supported, not by Aaron and Hur, but by the cross's arms.[†] Eyes of faith recognize in this scene a tremendous benediction.

The narrator in Arnulf of Leuven's poem is standing now, level with the Crucified. Only thus can he embrace Christ's hands. The postures we have so far considered, of prostration

---

[*] Cf. Psalm 23: 'The Lord is my Shepherd'.
[†] Exod. 14.21, 17.11f.

AD MANUS – TO THE HANDS

and kneeling, are reverential. There is a forthright quality in uprightness. Standing face to face with the humiliation of the incarnate Word, we confess at once, 'Behold the Man' and 'My Lord and my God'.[*]

As we fix our gaze on Jesus's wounded hands, we are made to confront that which, in the mystery of faith, is most mysterious: the freely chosen patience of Omnipotence, the paralysis of motion's Source. It is good to recall this image whenever we feel our hands are tied and we are tempted to despair, mistakenly supposing that only by *doing* something do we exist and act.

I once read the confidential account of a contemplative nun suffering from motor neurone disease. A woman of faith, she received the diagnosis level-headedly, consoling those who ostensibly came to comfort her. The relentless progress of the disease involved nonetheless epistemic readjustment. As her physical ability to act on the world diminished and she retreated, like a fresh-water mussel engaged in producing a fine pearl, into herself, her notion of who she was with regard to everything and everyone else altered. I remember a metaphor from her account, which she dictated to one of her sisters. She said something like this – having lost the text I am citing from memory: 'So far I have been paddling my life's canoe in a shielded forest lake, rejoicing in the setting's peaceful beauty. Now my boat is seized by the current. I no longer control its course. I am rushed along unknown, surprising shores. All I can do is to hold on, and somehow try to enjoy the ride.'

---

[*] Cf. Jn 19.5, 20.28.

I encountered this singular destiny early in my monastic life. At first I wondered whether this incongruous metaphor spelt sarcasm or even an expression of rage. Then, however, I understood that it speaks with the voice of a soul so convinced of God's goodness that even extreme paralysis is received as a gift in the certainty that somewhere, underneath it, there will be a blessing spent by the everlasting arms, and that meanwhile none too great a fuss should be made.

The more I reflect on it, the more I find in this confession an image, even an exegesis, of Jesus's outstretched arms on Calvary. It is a cause for wonder that here, in this arrested state, he utters a supremely dynamic intent, saying, 'Father, into your hands I commend my spirit.' Into your *hands*.[*]

Theology teaches that God's hands were never more active than when fastened to the wood of the tree, 'punctured by nails', causing blood to flow 'as the price of a great salvation'. This is a lesson to be pondered often and in silence.

Arnulf's meditation reveals a profoundly eucharistic sensibility. This is as you would expect from a Cistercian. In the third stanza of this section, his heart longs to be touched by the Saviour's blood-purpled hands. His mouth would drink 'drops of your blood that was shed'. Presupposed is the kind of associative thinking we find centuries later in the paintings of Fra Angelico or Giotto, where angels flutter around the cross holding chalices, collecting the same Precious Blood that is really present on the altar at Mass. We are reminded of the simultaneity of Christ's sacrifice and sacramental practice, for, as the priest prays over the bread and wine on

---

[*] Lk. 23.46.

Maundy Thursday, 'whenever the memorial of this sacrifice is celebrated the work of our redemption is accomplished.'[*]

Another striking image picked up and developed in the text is that of Christ's broadness: 'You show yourself broad.' His crucified hands are conceived of as extended in a universal embrace excluding no-one. Even as St Paul strained onwards and outwards, urged by Christ's love,[†] we see Jesus, who loved his own to the end,[‡] in some way the victim of his own philanthropy. He desired to gather Jerusalem's children 'together as a hen gathers her brood under her wings'.[§] On the cross he shows himself helplessly open-armed, emboldening us, hard-hearted lookers-on, to pray, 'Draw my senses towards you . . . conform me to your outstretched arms.'

The motif of broadness goes even further, though. Again and again in the Hebrew Bible, a contrast is drawn between narrow places in which it is dreadful to live (the Latin for 'narrowness', '*angustia*', gives us 'anguish') and broad spaces of happiness. In the twenty-sixth chapter of Genesis, which speaks of Isaac's return from Philistine Gerar, an Egypt in miniature, after time spent there to avoid another 'famine in the land', we find him engaged in his signature activity: the re-digging of wells 'dug in the days of Abraham his father' but since filled with earth by Philistines who did not

---

[*] From the offertory prayer of the Evening Mass of Maundy Thursday: 'Concede nobis, quaesumus, Domine, haec digne frequentare mysteria, quia, quoties huius hostiae commemoratio celebratur, opus nostrae redemptionis exercetur.'
[†] 2 Cor. 5.14.
[‡] Jn 13.1.
[§] Lk. 13.34.

want Isaac's flocks to thrive. Having quarrelled over many of these wells with herders of Gerar, he came upon one over which there was no dispute, 'so he called it "Broadness" [in Hebrew *Rehoboth*, in the Vulgate, *Latitudo*], saying, "Now the Lord has made room for us all, and we shall be fruitful in the land."'[*] Christ's open arms likewise indicate a broad space within which there is no need to compete to belong, where all can find stability and repose.

To thrive there, we must conform ourselves to the self-giving in charity of which Christ's arms speak. The prayers formulated on our behalf are radical: 'Let my ability, my knowledge, my will,/serve the cause of your cross'; 'Draw me to the cross's victory,/and put an end to my vices.' Anyone who would be held safe by Jesus's hands must relinquish any truck with wickedness and moral compromise, 'lest the righteous put forth their hands to do wrong'.[†] The same Lord who displays, on the cross, unconditional love sternly said: 'If your right hand causes you to sin, cut it off and throw it away.'[‡] The gravity of throwing the Lord's hand off, the grief we thereby cause ourselves and others, is graver than we tend to realize.

Lord Jesus, hold me gently but securely in your hand, form me by your design, make me beautiful and free. Preserve me from all underhand tricks. Let me not forget the wounds in your palms, pledges of a love I pray will ever more astound me.

---

[*] Gen. 26.1, 17–22.
[†] Psalm 125.3.
[‡] Mt. 5.30.

Ad latus – To the Side

Salve, Jesu, summe bonus
Ad parcendum nimis pronus:
Membra tua macilenta
Quam acerbe sunt distenta
   In ramo crucis torrida!

Salve, latus Salvatoris,
In quo latet mel dulcoris,
In quo patet vis amoris
Ex quo scatet fons cruoris,
   Qui corda lavat sordida.

Ecce tibi appropinquo,
Parce, Jesu, si delinquo:
Verecunda quidem fronte,
Ad te tamen veni sponte,
   Scrutari tua vulnera.

Salve, mitis apertura,
De qua manat vena pura,
Porta patens et profunda
Super rosam rubicunda
   Medela salutifera.

Odor tuus super vinum,
Virus pellens serpentinum;
Potus tuus, potus vitae:
Qui sititis, huc venite,
   Tu dulce vulnus aperi.

AD LATUS — TO THE SIDE

Hail, Jesus, supremely good,
most inclined to spare us.
Bitterly distended
are your gaunt members
parched on the cross-bough.

Hail, side of the Saviour in which
sweet honey is concealed, in which
love's strength is revealed, from which
a fount of blood gushes forth
to cleanse sordid hearts.

See, I approach you; spare me,
Jesus, if in so doing I trespass:
my brow is bashful, yet
I come before you of my own accord
to investigate your wounds.

Hail, modest breach from which
a pure course flows: you are
an open, unbounded doorway,
redder than any rose,
a saving remedy.

Your perfume surpasses that of wine.
It expels the serpent's poison:
your potion is the potion of life.
All you who thirst, come here!
Open, side of Christ, your sweet wound!

Plaga rubens, aperire.
Fac cor meum te sentire,
Sine me in te transire,
Vellem totus introire;
    Pulsanti pande pauperi.

Ore meo te contingo,
Et ardenter ad me stringo:
In te meum cor intingo,
Et ferventi corde lingo;
    Me totum in te trajice.

O quam dulcis sapor iste!
Qui te gustat, Jesu Christe,
Tuo victus a dulcore,
Mori posset prae amore,
    Te unum amans unice.

In hac fossa me reconde,
Infer meum cor profunde,
Ubi latens incalescat,
Et in pace conquiescat,
    Nec prorsus quemquam timeat.

Hora mortis meus flatus
Intret, Jesu, tuum latus,
Hinc exspirans in te vadat;
Ne hunc leo trux invadat,
    Sed apud te permaneat.

AD LATUS – TO THE SIDE

Open up, you blushing wound.
Sensitize my heart to you.
Let me fix my dwelling in you:
I wish to enter you wholly.
Open to the poor man knocking at the door.

I touch you with my mouth.
Ardently I pull you to myself.
I immerse my heart in you, lapping up
as much as I can with my fervent heart.
Draw me wholly into yourself.

How sweet this savour is!
One who tastes you, Jesus Christ,
might as well die for love,
vanquished by your sweetness,
loving you alone singularly.

Hide me away in this dug trench.
Carry my heart within its depth,
to where, concealed, it may be warmed,
to where it may find perfect rest in peace,
no more to fear anyone at all.

At the hour of my death, Jesus,
may my spirit gain access to your side.
Expiring there, may it enter into you,
lest the savage lion, here, claim it for itself.
Let it stay forever where you are.

The piercing of Jesus's side is recounted in the Fourth Gospel just after the words, 'It is accomplished.'

> Since it was the day of Preparation, in order to prevent the bodies from remaining on the cross on the sabbath (for that sabbath was a high day), the Jews asked Pilate that their legs might be broken, and that they might be taken away. So the soldiers came and broke the legs of the first, and of the other who had been crucified with him; but when they came to Jesus and saw that he was already dead, they did not break his legs. But one of the soldiers pierced his side with a lance, and at once there came out blood and water. He who saw it has borne witness – his testimony is true, and he knows that he tells the truth – that you also may believe. For these things took place that the Scripture might be fulfilled, 'Not a bone of him shall be broken.' And again another Scripture says, 'They shall look on him whom they have pierced.'*

The infliction of Christ's first four wounds, to his hands and feet, is ascribed to a collective entity, a faceless 'they'.[†] The fifth wound is wrought by a precise individual, 'one of the soldiers'. Christian imagination seized on this fact and rhapsodized on the subsequent fate of this man, whom tradition calls Longinus, a common enough name probably derived in this circumstance, by means of associative onomatopoeia, from the Greek word for a lance, *longchē*.

---

*Jn 19.31–7.
[†]As in Lk. 23.33: 'When they came to the place that is called the Skull, they crucified Jesus there with the other criminals.'

AD LATUS — TO THE SIDE

Mention is made of Longinus in an apocryphal text first extant in the sixth century known as *The Letter of Herod to Pilate*. The letter tells a moralizing tale. People get the just wages for their works already in this world without having to await the formalities of the Last Judgement. Herod's daughter loses her head. We are told it was pulled off her body by her mother in a vain attempt to rescue the child from drowning in a flood: implicit retribution for her part in the beheading of the Baptist. The king himself is eaten alive by worms, 'since I did so many evil things against [Jesus] and against John the Baptist'.

The author mixes up two biblical Herods, Agrippa and Antipas. He conflates destinies. But that is beside the point. The *Letter* is of interest not as a putative source of facts, but as a witness to early Christian notions of God's work of redemption.

The letter concludes with some words about Longinus. As soon as he had pierced the Saviour's side, we are told, an angel translated him from Calvary to the proverbial wilderness beyond the Jordan. The angel imprisoned him there in a cave, stretching him out on the ground. A ghastly fate awaited him: 'a lion was assigned to come forth at night and to destroy his body until dawn.' The lion would slink away at sunrise. Longinus's body would wondrously heal during the day, only for the procedure to resume at dusk. 'This is the punishment he receives until the Second Coming of Christ.'*

Who knows whether there is resonance of such lore in the *Rhythmica oratio*, in the prayer to find refuge, at death's

---

* *The Apocryphal Gospels: Texts and Translations*, ed. and trans. Bart D. Ehrman and Zlatko Pleše (Oxford: Oxford University Press, 2011), pp. 524–7.

hour, in Christ's side wound, 'lest the savage lion, here, claim [my spirit] for itself'? The lion's mouth is in any case a biblical shorthand for faith's enemy, harking back to the enclosure of Daniel in the lions' den;[*] canonized by way of aspiration in the Second Letter to Timothy, 'as I was rescued from the lion's mouth, the Lord will rescue me from every evil attack';[†] then woven into the Offertory chant of the Church's *Requiem* Mass: 'Free them from the lion's mouth lest the netherworld consume them.'[‡] Evident in the poem is symbolic opposition between Christ's protecting wound and the prospect of devouring destruction.

Later Christian tradition saw Longinus more benignly. The *Legenda Aurea*, compiled a generation after Arnulf of Leuven's death, containing stories told during his lifetime, makes of the Roman soldier a paradigm of penitence. In Caxton's resonant fifteenth-century rendering, lightly touched up:

> Some say that when he smote our Lord with the spear in the side, the precious blood avaled by the shaft of the spear upon his hands, and of adventure with his hands he touched his eyes, and anon he that had been tofore blind saw anon clearly, wherefore he refused all chivalry and abode with the apostles, of whom he was taught and christened, and after, he abandoned him to lead an holy

---

[*] Dan. 6.16–24.
[†] 2 Tim. 4.17.
[‡] The Latin text can be found in any Missal, Gradual or Mozart *Requiem* CD booklet.

AD LATUS – TO THE SIDE

life in doing alms and in keeping the life of a monk about 38 years in Caesarea and in Cappadocia, and by his words and his example many men converted he to the faith of Christ.[*]

The motif of blindness healed makes us think of a corresponding miracle, one that took place just before Christ's ascent to Jerusalem.

In the Synoptic Gospels, Jesus, going up to undergo his passion, is intercepted near Jericho by blind Bartimaeus, a beggar. Jesus summons him and asks: 'What would you have me do for you?' The blind man answers: 'Lord, that I may see!' Bartimaeus's sight is restored to him forthwith 'and he followed him on the road'.[†]

The account recurs with minor variations (in Matthew there are two beggars, not one) in all three Gospels at the same crucial point in the story. This indicates both a strong historical tradition and symbolic import. While the morally blind, stuck in prejudice, fail to recognize Jesus's signs and plot his demise,[‡] the physically blind recognize his Lordship. Their sight restored, they desire but one thing: to remain with him and to follow him wherever he goes.

The reader is led to reflect on the life-giving, illuminating power of Jesus's teaching, presence and saving sacrifice.

---

[*] *The Golden Legend or Lives of the Saints as Englished by William Caxton*, 7 vols. ed. F. S. Ellis (London: Dent, 1900), III, 70.
[†] Mk 10.46–52, cf. Mt. 20.29–34 and Lk. 18.35–43.
[‡] See for instance Jn 9 and Mt. 23.26.

The speculation that Longinus had been blind expands the paradigm. Jesus's power to heal is not curtailed by his death on the cross. On the contrary. Channelled into a sacramental economy, it is universalized, rendered accessible and effective wherever the sacred mysteries are celebrated.

The topos of a blindness healed by contact with sanctified blood spread into hagiography. It became a privileged means by which to render explicit a martyr's Christlikeness. As such we find it stressed, for example, in the chronicles of the royal martyrs Saints Olav and Erik. The suspected holiness of both is proved when a blind person, in each case a disreputable specimen, by accident touches the martyr's blood, then puts a hand to his or her own face, and once again sees.

In the *Legenda Aurea* Longinus goes on to become an illuminator of men. He is presented as a doughty confessor and exorcist as well as, both before and after death, an effective intercessor. During a showdown in Cappadocia, where the wicked 'provost' Octavian, a Roman official, would force him to sacrifice to idols, Longinus besought God to take away his adversary's sight to preserve him from his own wicked zeal. Octavian nonetheless succeeded in striking off Longinus's head, only to collapse on the martyr's body weeping tears of repentance. His sight was restored through the dead man's prayers, upon which Octavian 'believed in Jesu Christ and abode in the company of Christian men, and thanked God, and died in good estate'.

These two stories, so different in character, bring out complementary aspects of the wound in Jesus's side. The earlier, Greek source focuses on the holiness of the Crucified.

AD LATUS – TO THE SIDE

The doing of deliberate violence to God, be it motivated humanely – the soldiers went about their business to put sufferers out of their misery – was so enormous that preternatural punishment was thought to be called for.

The Letter of Herod to Pilate makes sense in the light of a Scriptural story of something that took place when David, anointed king of all Israel, brought the ark of the covenant out of Abinadab's house on the hill, its place of exile, into Jerusalem, where the temple would arise around it. The ark was carried on an ox cart while David and all Israel 'danced before the Lord', the ark being understood as a tabernacle carrying God's Real Presence, 'with all their might, with songs and lyres and harps and tambourines and castanets and cymbals'.

One imagines the noise. The hubbub made the oxen jumpy. At one point Uzzah, one of Abinadab's sons who accompanied the cart, 'reached out his hand to the ark of God and took hold of it, for the oxen shook it'. His intention was to prop it up in an awkward bend to prevent it from sliding off. There was no shade of blasphemy in his action. Yet 'the anger of the Lord was kindled against Uzzah; and God smote him there because he put forth his hand to the ark.'

A mixture of emotions seized David as he witnessed what was going on. On the one hand he was cross with God for striking Uzzah, who seemed to him beyond reproach; on the other hand he was in awe of God's holiness with which he had insufficiently reckoned. The object before which he had danced with abandon to the rhythm of frenzied castanets was not, it dawned on him, a manageable totem;

it was a vehicle of judgement intolerant even of accidental profanation.

David exclaimed: 'How can the ark of the Lord come into my care?' He saw that to be in God's proximity is not tantamount to being safe. He decided there and then to park the ark in the house of Obed-Edom, the Gittite, while he went back to his palace to consider options. It took David three months of reflection to muster up courage to fetch the ark anew and set it in its place, to bring it home.[*]

What the ark once prefigured is realized in Jesus. We have considered how the veil before the Holy of Holies was rent when, a stone's throw outside the city, Christ expired: '*anticuum documentum novo cedat ritui*'.[†] For a mind immersed in Old Testament imagery, Longinus's violation of Christ's body was like a prising open of the ark to lay grubby hands on divine realities.

Not for nothing is there a parallel between the chastisement meted out to Longinus and that endured, in Greek myth, by Prometheus after his attempt to steal Olympian fire. According to Hesiod, Prometheus was bound, then, to a rock where an eagle, the emblem of Zeus, would alight and pick at his liver by day, only for the liver to grow back overnight, to perpetuate the hero's agony.[‡]

---

[*] 2 Sam. 6.1–19.
[†] A line from the hymn '*Pange Lingua*' composed by St Thomas Aquinas for the feast of Corpus Christi and customarily sung at Benediction, when the sacrament of Christ's Body is exposed for adoration: 'Let the ancient dispensation yield to the new rite.'
[‡] See Hesiod's *Theogony*, lines 520–7.

In Christian tradition, the lion is a symbol of Christ. The connection is made in the Apocalypse, where John hears an elder proclaim: 'See, the Lion of the tribe of Judah, the Root of David, has conquered, so that he can open the scroll and its seven seals.'[*] The fate of Longinus in the sixth-century Greek account reminds us that the King who conquered on Calvary is also our Judge, holy and just. We shall answer before him for our deeds. A desecration or wounding of his body, be it in the species of bread or in mystery as the body of the Church, is no trifling matter.

The medieval Latin perspective of the *Legenda Aurea* is different. It sets out from a pondered, eucharistic understanding of what takes place when the Lord's side is opened. Presupposed is a sensibility with biblical roots in the First Epistle of John, which interprets the Johannine passion narrative. In the last paragraphs before the salutations, John speaks of the way in which a Christian becomes a child of God through faith in 'a victory that conquers the world'. He asks: 'Who is it that conquers the world?' He then provides the answer: 'He who believes that Jesus is the Son of God'; that is, who makes his own the confession that was uttered at the foot of the cross by the centurion we read of in the Gospel of Matthew, a man so overwhelmed by the earthquake, the opening of tombs, and all that took place when Jesus breathed his last that he cried out: 'Truly this man was God's Son.'[†]

---

[*] Rev. 5.5.
[†] Mt. 27.54.

A strand of tradition came to identify this centurion as, precisely, Longinus,[*] lodging within the parameters of biography a theological connection which the First Epistle of John goes on to make as it says about the Son of God:

> This is he who came by water and blood, Jesus Christ, not with the water only but with the water and the blood. And the Spirit is the witness, because the Spirit is the truth. There are three witnesses, the Spirit, the water and the blood; and these three agree . . . God gave us eternal life, and this life is in his Son. He who has the Son has life; he who has not the Son of God has not life.[†]

On this reading, the piercing of Christ's side to release the blood and water can be construed as a priestly gesture, symbolically reminiscent of the ritual performed by Aaron on the annual Day of Atonement when, alone of all the people, he entered the holy of holies to sprinkle blood upon the mercy-seat, thus letting a river of mercy pour forth upon expectant Israel.[‡]

The Fathers followed this thought-current when they presented the piercing of Christ's side as the calling-into-being of the Church. They understood the water and blood as representations of Baptism and the Eucharist, of recreation and transfiguration. Then they drew a symbolic

---

[*] It is referred to in Butler's *Lives of the Saints* under 15 March, where relevant literature is listed.
[†] 1 Jn 5.6–12.
[‡] Lev. 16.15–19.

line from the story of the lance to the promise Christ makes earlier in John's Gospel, when he stands in the temple on the last day of the festival of Booths and cries out:

> 'If any one thirst, let him come to me and drink. He who believes in me, as the Scripture has said, "Out of his heart shall flow rivers of living water".' Now this he said about the Spirit, which those who believed in him were to receive; for as yet the Spirit had not been given, because Jesus was not yet glorified.[*]

The side-wound seen in this context is gracious. It enables an effusion of glory, the rebirth of man in the baptistery and the stilling of his hunger on the altar. Made new in the Spirit, fed with spiritual food, human nature reveals its potential, pouring forth 'rivers of living water' in an analogy to Christ's gift on Calvary.[†]

Against this background we can understand the otherwise troubling images of eating and drinking that occur through Arnulf's poem, especially in this section. When he speaks of 'lapping up' the effluence from Christ's side, whose perfume exceeds that of wine, the association is eucharistic. It posits in Christ's physical wound the source of sacramental, mystical grace that through the Church satisfies the existential thirst of humankind. The cry, 'All you who thirst, come here!',

---

[*] Jn 7.37–9.
[†] A wonderful and monumentally learned account of this vast tradition can be found in Hugo Rahner's *Symbole der Kirche: Die Ekklesiologie der Väter* (Salzburg: Müller, 1964), notably in Part III, '*Flumina de ventre Christi*: Die patristische Auslegung von Joh. 7.37–8'.

recalls both the line from Isaiah, 'Ho, everyone who thirsts, come to the waters; and he who has no money, come, buy and eat!',[*] and the words of Jesus in the temple, just cited.

The motif of 'sweetness' recurs combined with that of honey, the standard sweetener of the ancient Mediterranean world, ignorant of sugar. The description of the Promised Land as a land flowing 'with milk and honey' is used throughout the Pentateuch as an attraction to keep the indolent moving.[†]

When Arnulf refers to the 'side of the Saviour in which/ sweet honey is concealed', however, the reference is more specific. It takes us to one of the grandest orations in all of Scripture, the 'song' Moses sings to Israel's remnant at the end of Deuteronomy, re-reading the people's long journey, and his own life, in the light of eternity. Israel's provident Lord is spoken of in terms of paradox to let us appreciate his unpredictable being and agency. He is 'the Rock' whose works are perfect, the foundation and sole source of stability in a changing world. At the same time he is 'an Eagle' flying on the wings of the wind, elegant and light, shielding Israel, caring for him, guarding him 'as the apple of his eye'. 'Like an eagle that stirs up its nest, fluttering over its young, spreading out its wings, catching them, bearing them on its pinions', so the Lord led Israel through howling wastes, setting him at last 'atop the heights of the land' where he is

---

[*] Isa. 55.1.
[†] The first occurrence is in Exod. 3.8.

AD LATUS — TO THE SIDE

fed 'with the produce of the field; he made him suck honey out of the rock, and oil out of the flinty rock.'[*]

The hope that for ancient Israel was rooted in mellifluous Palestine is for the Church 'the Israel of God',[†] rooted in God's Son: from his fullness we receive grace upon grace.[‡] Christ's saving passion is the goal of the Christian exodus: each year we re-read the story of Israel's wilderness journey to prepare for Easter. The fulfilment that in Deuteronomy is found 'atop the heights of the land' is transferred to the glory of Christ's Pasch. Jesus's steadfastness, his acceptance of the Father's chalice and his refusal to heed the taunting crowd's cry, 'Let him come down from the cross, and we shall believe,'[§] display rocklike solidity, while the eagle's pinions are but an inadequate sign of the grace with which he arose out of death to ascend to a shareable reality of life eternal. To identify Christ's side-wound as the source of honey destined to flow through the land of resurrection promise, flooding it with consolation, is to view the sacred passion eschatologically, finding in it the hermeneutical key to a millennial salvation history.

The affective warmth of this section of the *Rhythmica oratio* displays personal devotion and intense hope. Though not explicitly referred to, a line from the Song of Songs, the medieval Cistercians' favourite biblical text, is never far from the surface: 'O my dove, in the clefts of the rock,

---

[*]Moses's song takes up nearly all of Deut. 32.
[†]Gal. 6.16.
[‡]Cf. Jn 1.16.
[§]Mt. 26.39–42, 27.42.

in the covert of the cliff, let me see your face, let me hear your voice, for your voice is sweet, and your face is lovely.'[*] St Bernard of Clairvaux once wrote about this passage: 'everything belonging to the earth is shifting and unstable; but our Rock is in heaven, and from it all our safety and stability derive. The rock is a refuge for the conies, and where indeed are there complete security and rest for us frail men, save in the Saviour's Wounds?'[†] The wound in Christ's side is our point of entry into an experience of redemption. It is an inexhaustible source of grace for the ungracious, liquefying hardened hearts.

> Lord Jesus, may I never afflict your body, present to me in mystery through your Church. Let me draw sanctifying strength from the blood and water that pour forth from your side, so to shelter sweetly in the cleft of the one true, saving Rock.

---

[*] Song. 2.14.
[†] *Saint Bernard on the Song of Songs: Sermones in Cantica Canticorum*, trans. and ed. A Religious of the CSMV (London: Mowbray, 1952), Sermon XXVIII, pp. 194–5.

Ad pectus – To the Breast

Salve, salus mea Deus,
Jesu dulcis amor meus:
Salve, pectus reverendum,
Cum tremore contingendum
    Amoris domicilium.

Ave, thronus Trinitatis,
Arca latae charitatis,
Firmamentum infirmatis,
Pax et pausa fatigatis,
    Humilium triclinium.

Salve, Jesu reverende,
Digne semper inquirende;
Me praesentem hic attende,
Accedentem me succende,
    Praecordiali gratia.

Pectus mihi confer mundum,
Ardens, pium, gemebundum,
Voluntatem abnegatam,
Tibi semper conformatam,
    Juncta virtutum copia.

Jesu dulcis, pastor pie,
Fili Dei et Mariae,
Largo fonte tui cordis,
Foeditatem meae sordis,
    Benigne pater, dilue.

AD PECTUS – TO THE BREAST

Hail, my God and salvation,
Jesus, my sweet love.
Hail, awe-inspiring breast.
Only with trembling dare I touch you.
You are love's home.

Hail, throne of the Trinity and
ark of broad charity,
firm ground for the infirm,
peace and rest for the weary,
dining-couch of the humble.

Jesus, I salute and revere you.
You are always worthy to be sought.
Attend to me, present here.
As I come to you, set me on fire
with intimate grace

Grant me a breast that is pure,
ardent, faithful, full of sighs.
Make my will unselfish:
conform it to your will, to be
at one with the store of all virtue.

Sweet Jesus, faithful shepherd,
Son of God and Mary's Son,
from your heart's broad wellspring
cleanse, kind father, that in me
which is squalid and foul.

Ave, splendor et figura
Summi Dei genitura,
De thesauris tuis plenis
Desolatis et egenis
   Munus clementer perflue.

Dulcis Jesu Christi pectus,
Tuo fiam dono rectus,
Absolutus a peccatis,
Ardens igne charitatis
   Ut semper te recogitem.

Tu abyssus es sophiae,
Angelorum harmoniae
Te collaudant, ex te fluxit
Quod Joannes cubans suxit:
   In te fac ut inhabitem.

Ave, fons benignitatis,
Plenitudo deitatis
Corporalis in te manet:
Vanitatem in me sanet
   Quod tu confers consilium.

Ave, verum templum Dei;
Precor, miserere mei:
Tu totius arca boni,
Fac electis me apponi,
   Vas dives, Deus omnium.

AD PECTUS – TO THE BREAST

Hail, splendour and figure of
God most high, called to be born a man.
From your brimful treasure-chests
pour out your gift with mercy
on the hopeless and poor.

Sweet breast of Christ Jesus,
let me by your gift stand upright,
absolved from sin,
on fire with charity's flame,
with you in my constant thoughts.

You are the abyss of wisdom.
Angelic harmonies praise you.
Your effluence is what
John, leaning on you, imbibed.
Let me find my home in you.

Hail, fount of kindness.
In you the fullness of Deity
dwells bodily.
I pray that your counsel will
heal all the vanity I carry.

Hail, true sanctuary of God.
Pray, have mercy on me!
You are the ark of all that is good.
Place me alongside the elect,
splendid vessel, God of all.

In terms of correspondence to recorded events, the section *Ad pectus* is the least obvious in this meditation on the passion. The other examined parts of Christ's body, the hands and feet, the knees and side, the heart and head, sustain particular wounds during the course of crucifixion. The breast meanwhile is generic, not so much a body part as a physical region containing affected organs.

The author brings this spaciousness out in his choice of epithets. He stresses the breast's capacity as 'love's home', 'ark of charity', 'fountain of kindness', 'temple of God' and so forth. To these high metaphors a specific, circumstantial reference is joined. Jesus's breast is described as 'dining-couch of the humble'. On this couch John reclined while he sucked up the wisdom erupting from within it. Alluded to here is a scene from the last supper as it is described in the Gospel of John.[*]

Knowing 'that his hour had come to depart out of this world to the Father', Jesus had washed the apostles' feet, a gesture containing in germ a new and eternal commandment to love as he loves – selflessly, in a posture of service, sacrificially and 'to the end'. The washing had concluded with the troubling assertion, 'You are clean, though not all of you.' The prospect of Judas's betrayal is made explicit.

An Old Testament prophecy is cited, a verse from Psalm 41. In the Gospel it is given thus: 'He who ate my bread has lifted his heel against me.' If we look up the Hebrew text of the Psalm, we shall find this person portrayed as *ish shlomi*, 'the man of my peace', that is, 'the one with whom

---

[*] The references that follow are all from the Gospel's thirteenth chapter.

AD PECTUS – TO THE BREAST

I had made a compact of peace' and in whom, so the verse carries on, 'I had hoped.'* The Revised Standard Version offers a touching paraphrase, speaking of 'my bosom friend in whom I trusted'. This choice of words is memorable in the light of the continued Gospel text, in which Jesus helps the Twelve to reflect on the nature of betrayal and on the traitor's identity:

> When Jesus had thus spoken, he was troubled in spirit, and testified, 'Truly, truly, I say to you, one of you will betray me.' The disciples looked at one another, uncertain of whom he spoke. One of his disciples, whom Jesus loved, was lying close to the breast of Jesus; so Simon Peter beckoned to him and said, 'Tell us who it is of whom he speaks.' So lying thus, close to the breast of Jesus, he said to him, 'Lord, who is it?' Jesus answered, 'It is he to whom I shall give this morsel when I have dipped it.' So when he had dipped the morsel, he gave it to Judas, the son of Simon Iscariot. Then after the morsel, Satan entered into him. Jesus said to him, 'What you are going to do, do quickly.' Now no one at the table knew why he said this to him. Some thought that, because Judas had the money box, Jesus was telling him, 'Buy what we need for the feast'; or, that he should give something to the poor. So, after receiving the morsel, he immediately went out; and it was night.

---

*Psalm 41.9 in the RSV, 41.10 in the Hebrew.

The intimate image of John reclining on Jesus's breast is offset by the cold shadow that overhangs the treachery of Judas, a dark intention which physical night fittingly absorbs when the keeper of the apostolic purse, madly unaware of the self-destructive end of the path he chooses, departs. For had not this man, too, been a 'bosom friend', one for whom it had been possible and somehow normal to lean on Christ's breast? The resonance of the Psalm verse fills the scene with sadness.

The title 'beloved disciple' attaches to the narrating voice in the Gospel of John. It is not used throughout the text, however; only in its final chapters. We find it here for the first time.[*] Then it reappears at significant junctures.

It is next used when Jesus, in agony, entrusts his mother: 'When Jesus saw his mother and the disciple whom he loved standing beside her, he said to his mother, "Woman, this is your son". Then he said to the disciple, "Here is your mother".'[†] It is used again when Mary Magdalene early on Easter Sunday, 'while it was still dark', finds Jesus's tomb, sealed on Friday, standing open. 'She ran and went to Simon Peter and the other disciple, the one whom Jesus loved, and said to them, "They have taken the Lord away".' The two men set off together to the burial site, 'but the other disciple outran Peter and reached the tomb first'. Peering in, he saw the grave clothes lying on the floor, every bit as redundant as those of Lazarus had lain before a similar tomb in Bethany some months before, after the accomplishment of

---

[*] In Jn 13.23.
[†] Jn 19.26f.

a 'sign' whose full significance now dawns. Peter, entrusted with the privilege and grace of primacy, may have entered the tomb first, but it was 'the other disciple' who first 'saw and believed'.[*] The two men engage in a similar contest of confession some time later, on the Sea of Tiberias, when Christ appears on the shore 'and the disciple whom Jesus loved said to Peter, "It is the Lord"'. On hearing this Peter, stripped of both clothes and self-confidence, jumped into the sea, no longer knowing quite what was required of him.[†] A final glimpse of the 'beloved disciple' is caught in the Gospel's closing vignette. At that point he follows Christ silently, observing what the Lord does and says, not intruding, simply staying close, heeding the call to 'abide' with him. 'This,' we are told, 'is the disciple who is testifying to these things and has written them, and we know that his testimony is true.'[‡]

The historical identity of the 'beloved disciple' has exercised exegetes for ages. It is legitimate to speculate, but there can be little doubt that authorial intent is to present him as the apostle whose name the Gospel bears. At the same time 'the beloved disciple' is emblematic. He is the true believer who bears witness so that others may believe and have life in Jesus's name.[§] He represents not merely a particular testimony, but a trajectory you and I may follow as members of Christ's great sacrament, his abiding,

---

[*] Jn 20.1–10, cf. 11.44.
[†] Jn 21.1–8.
[‡] Jn 21.20–4.
[§] Jn 20.31.

effective presence in the Spirit through the Church.[*] In this perspective, the junctures at which the 'beloved disciple' is referred to – as a graced participant in the Last Supper, as an adopted son of Mary, as witness to the cross and resurrection, as a follower of Jesus risen from the dead – are relieved of their exclusive embeddedness in time. They become shareable.

The *Rhythmica oratio* develops the theme of a communion transcending time and space by voicing in the name of every reader a desire to rest familiarly on Jesus's breast as John rested there. This is no passive state of careless spiritual bliss. It is an active preparation for discipleship. From this experience John drew the strength he needed to stand firm when the other ten remaining disciples ran; to face Christ's affliction in the noisy, stinking squalor of a public spectacle; to see a friend he loved suffer unspeakably; to embrace that friend's mother, whose grief had been foretold years before in terms of the violent but still inadequate image of a sword-blade piercing her soul;[†] to hear Jesus cry, first, 'I thirst', then 'It is finished'; then to see him bow his head and give up his spirit.[‡]

In the upper room, Jesus knew what lay ahead of him.[§] The story moves fast from this point on. Within a couple

---

[*] The nature of the Church as sacrament is stressed in paragraph one of the Second Vatican Council's constitution *Lumen Gentium*: 'the Church is in Christ like a sacrament or as a sign and instrument both of a very closely knit union with God and of the unity of the whole human race.'
[†] Lk. 2.35.
[‡] Jn 19.25–30.
[§] Jn 13.1.

AD PECTUS — TO THE BREAST

of hours we find him in Gethsemane praying that the cup of sacrifice might pass, seized by such anguish that 'his sweat became like real drops of blood falling down on the ground'.[*] Presentiments of agony will have been alive in his breast, tightening it, at the supper as he spoke of his imminent handing-over into murderous hands. John, a man of consummate sensibility, will not have missed this surge of emotions, which evidenced the concreteness of the reality he later affirmed as a theological axiom: the Word did indeed *become flesh*, susceptible to all that which flesh in this world is prone to undergo. The incarnate Logos knew within his breast the clinging descent of despair's nocturnal shroud yet, being Light, was unovercome by it.[†] John leant upon the seat within which this drama, at once human and metaphysical, was being played out.

To perceive that someone we love and for whom we feel responsible is subject to great suffering while there is nothing, absolutely nothing we can do to help is a tremendous aspect of the human condition. The only constructive option open to us in such cases is that of compassion, a humbly determined resolve to remain close to the other in their state of extremity.

We might ask ourselves whether we are prepared to bear and, insofar as we are able, share what stirs in the Saviour's breast inhabited by the world's tragedy, instantiated here in the betrayal of a friend? The question is pertinent as

---

[*] Lk. 22.41–4.
[†] Cf. the whole thrust of the Johannine Prologue, Jn 1–18.

we consider John's resting there, attentive and receptive, listening to God's rushing heartbeat.

For the friend in whose bosom John reclines is divine. This affirmation is structural to John's whole Gospel; yet we easily forget it. Origen, the eagle-eyed, was less liable to such neglect. He writes in his commentary on the Fourth Gospel:

> John, reclining on the Word and resting on more mystical things, was reclining in the bosom of the Word, analogous to the Word being in the bosom of the Father, according to the statement, 'The only-begotten God who is in the bosom of the Father, he has declared him.'[*]

Could this unforgettable image from John's Prologue – of the Son in the Father's bosom – have formed in the evangelist's mind while he himself reclined in the bosom of the Son at the supper prefiguring his saving passion? The thought is pure conjecture; but it is surely not implausible.

As we put ourselves in John's place and make his Christological confession ours close to Christ's breast, let us soberly remember what happens next in the Gospel: Jesus dips a piece of bread and gives it to Judas saying, 'What you are going to do, do quickly.'[†] The thought is unbearable,

---

[*] At XXXII.264 in Origen's commentary, cited in the *Ancient Christian Commentary on Scripture*, 29 vols (Downers Grove: InterVarsity Press, 2001–5), New Testament series IV*b*, on John 11–21, ed. by Joel C. Elowsky, p. 104.
[†] Jn 13.27.

AD PECTUS – TO THE BREAST

but ineluctable: it *is* possible to rest on Jesus's breast as his bosom friend one moment, then to betray him the next.

An old troparion assigned for recitation at the moment of approaching holy communion, the moment in our sacramental life that most objectively resembles John's closeness to Jesus, puts words into our mouth that will never be superfluous:

> O Son of God, receive me today as a partaker of your mystic supper, for I shall not betray your mysteries to your enemies, nor will I give you a kiss as Judas did, but with the thief I will confess, 'Remember me, O Lord, when you come into your kingdom.'*

The Son of God is king. He is also priest. A sacerdotal strain runs through the Johannine corpus. It is subtly present in John's chronology of the passion. Different from that of the other three Gospels, it has Christ's crucifixion coincide with the sacrifice of paschal lambs in the temple. On the cross, Jesus shows himself at once victim and priest, the agent of his own oblation;† indeed, he is, as he declared before the chief priests, a new kind of temple,‡ embodying a novel

---

*This troparion, Τοῦ Δείπνου σου τοῦ μυστικοῦ σήμερον, which originally replaced the Cherubic Hymn on Maundy Thursday, was introduced into the liturgy under Emperor Justin II. See the article 'Cheroubikon' in *The Oxford Dictionary of Byzantium*, ed. Alexander P. Kazhdan (New York, Oxford: Oxford University Press, 1991).

†Cf. Jn 10.18: 'No one takes [my life] from me, but I lay it down of my own accord.'

‡Mk 14.58, cf. Rev. 21.22.

dispensation of sacrifice of which the ancient priestly order was a figure.

We find the New Testament's clearest exposition of a priestly christology in the Letter to the Hebrews. The author picks up a tantalizing thread from a Psalm of David. The Psalm announces the enthronement in Zion of a ruler unlike any other ruler known to man. The Lord says to him, 'from the womb before the dawn I begot you', then declares him ordained to the Bible's most archaic order of priesthood: 'You are a priest for ever according to the order of Melchizedek.' This ruler will face hosts of enemies. His 'sceptre of power' will not be universally acclaimed. He will 'drink from the brook by the wayside', that is, he will be brought low. But his humiliation serves a purpose of exaltation: 'therefore he will lift up his head'.[*]

The Fathers delighted in this concentrate of mystical predictions. It seemed to them evidently a prophecy of Christ's incarnation. His origin in the Father's bosom appears in the image of begetting before time, when the dawn was not yet. Christ's sacrifice makes sense of the providential marker held in the story of Melchizedek of Salem, prehistoric Jerusalem, to whom Abram, God's elect, paid a tithe when Melchizedek, 'priest of God Most High', brought out gifts of bread and wine.[†]

---

[*]Psalm 109/110 is expounded in chapter 5 of the Letter to the Hebrews. The Psalm verse about generation before the dawn is not found in modern English Bibles, translated from the Hebrew, but it is present in the Septuagint, which was the New Testament writers' Old Testament: ἐκ γαστρὸς πρὸ ἑωσφόρου ἐξεγέννησά σε (verse 3 in the Greek text).
[†]Gen. 14.18–20.

AD PECTUS – TO THE BREAST

Apart from the Davidic citation, Melchizedek had stayed all but unconsidered since patriarchal times, but the author of Hebrews (certain, like St Peter, that the prophets of old were entrusted with secrets 'serving not themselves but [us]' who are blessed to live 'in the last time', seeing clearly 'things into which angels long to look')[*] confidently spells out his role in salvation history. The name 'Melchizedek', he points out, means 'king of righteousness'. Since his kingdom was Salem, a name drawn from the same root as *shalom*, he can also be called 'king of peace'. 'He is without father or mother or genealogy, and has neither beginning of days nor end of life, but resembling the Son of God he continues a priest for ever.'[†] The brook in the Psalm's final verse was seen by the Fathers as a code for the human condition. Bending low to drink of it, God's Son became like us, imbibing our predicament and hope, assuming in our name the cup of God's wrath, his response to our rebellion, which he drained to the dregs.[‡] The ensuing lifting-up of our collective head is the net result of God's becoming man.

Drily summarized one point after another, this kind of typological reading can seem laboured, dull. Considered as a whole, however, and contemplated quietly it acquires with time irresistible conviction. Not for nothing does the Church prescribe the recitation of Psalm 110, the one expounded in Hebrews, each Sunday at vespers to introduce

---

[*] 1 Pet. 1.3–12.
[†] Heb. 7.1–3.
[‡] Cf. Psalm 75.8 and the evident reference to the 'cup' in Gethsemane, considered above.

the evening sacrifice of praise on the day of resurrection. I invite anyone unconvinced by the coincidence of Christocentric clues to consider one of the Western Church's sublimest engagements with this text, a work of theology in sound: George Friderich Handel's setting of it in the form of a *concert spirituel* first performed in Rome on the feast of Our Lady of Mount Carmel in 1707. No source has more deeply affected my overall understanding of this prophetic text than the soprano–contralto duet interpreting the Psalm's final verse: 'He will drink from the brook by the wayside; therefore he will lift up his head.' It gives a tonality that, once perceived, is unforgettable, allowing us to hear what the Son's self-emptying means.[*]

It harmonizes the synthesis of old and new that alone lets us grasp the eternal impact of God's saving work in Christ. As the Second Vatican Council stated:

> The principal purpose to which the plan of the old covenant was directed was to prepare for the coming of Christ, the redeemer of all and of the messianic kingdom, to announce this coming by prophecy, and to indicate its meaning through various types . . . God, the inspirer and author of both Testaments, wisely arranged that the New Testament be hidden in the Old and the Old be made manifest in the New. For, though Christ established the new covenant in His blood, still the books of the Old Testament with all their parts, caught up into the proclamation of the Gospel, acquire and show forth their

---

[*] Handel's *Dixit Dominus* is catalogued as HWV 232.

AD PECTUS — TO THE BREAST

full meaning in the New Testament and in turn shed light on it and explain it.[*]

Melchizedek, encountered by Abram, sung of by David, provides a type that permits us to grasp Christ's role as a 'great high priest who has passed through the heavens', who 'in every respect has been tested as we are, yet without sin'. On account of his sinlessness he has no need, like other high priests, 'to offer sacrifice day after day, first for his own sins, then for those of the people'. He did this 'once for all when he offered himself', perfecting the priestly orders of both Melchizedek and Aaron. In his body he brought a single, all-embracing oblation that stays forever present in the Church, not cyclically repeated but forever new each time it is offered.[†]

Awareness of Christ's priestly identity and task sheds additional light on his breast as we consider it biblically. I think of a passage from the twenty-eighth chapter of Exodus, which itemizes Aaron's 'glorious adornment', required for his entry into the tabernacle to face the mercy seat. The Septuagint calls this seat *hilastērion*, a term Paul would later use, in his letter to the Romans, as a designation for Christ, 'whom God', he wrote, 'put forward as a *hilastērion* by his blood'. The word can be understood as both the sacrifice and the place of atonement, indicating the totality of the oblation that sealed the new and eternal covenant.[‡]

---

[*] *Dei Verbum*, the Council's Dogmatic Constitution on Divine Revelation, nn. 15–16.
[†] I have developed this theme in the fourth chapter of my book *The Shattering of Loneliness* (London: Bloomsbury, 2018).
[‡] Rom. 3.25. The construction of the *hilastērion* is described in Exod. 25.17ff.

Foremost on the list of Aaron's priestly garments is his breastpiece. The specifications for confection read like a litany. It is to be made of gold, blue, purple and scarlet stuff, fine twined linen, a span in length and breadth.

> And you shall set in it four rows of stones. A row of sardius, topaz, and carbuncle shall be the first row; and the second row an emerald, a sapphire, and a diamond; and the third row a jacinth, an agate, and an amethyst; and the fourth row a beryl, an onyx, and a jasper; they shall be set in gold filigree. There shall be twelve stones with their names according to the names of the sons of Israel; they shall be like signets, each engraved with its name, for the twelve tribes.[*]

By putting on this singular garment, Aaron will always, each time he enters the holy place, bear Israel's sons' names on his breast in 'continual remembrance before the Lord'. They are to be lodged there together with the Urim and Thummim, priestly devices for obtaining oracles and for distributing judgement, 'thus Aaron shall bear the judgement of the people of Israel upon his heart'. He is to be a conduit recalling to the Lord Israel's needs and to Israel God's standard of justice.[†]

In the New Testament the apostles appear as successors to Jacob's sons, called to engender an *ecclesia* intended to embrace all humankind. In the Bible's last book,

---

[*] Exod. 28.15–21.
[†] Exod. 28.29–30.

the *Apocalypse*, we find this new humanity's home, the eschatological city of the New Jerusalem, surrounded by walls adorned in a way that recalls the high priest's breastplate uncannily: 'the first was jasper, the second sapphire, the third agate, the fourth emerald, the fifth onyx, the sixth carnelian, the seventh chrysolite, the eighth beryl, the ninth topaz, the tenth chrysoprase, the eleventh jacinth, the twelfth amethyst'. On the walls are 'the twelve names of the twelve apostles of the Lamb', corresponding to those of Jacob's sons engraved on the gems of Aaron's garment.[*]

To be a citizen of the New Jerusalem is to exist by conflating these two models of design: that of the breastplate and that of the city. It is to reside within the very breast of him who perfected and fulfilled what Aaron had foreshadowed. It is to be configured to him who was perfectly obedient to the Father's will, pouring himself out in love, thus restoring man's innocence.

Subsisting within the breastplate, building up the city whose light is the Lamb,[†] we have the consolation of being remembered in Christ's heart. At the same time we are agents of remembrance in his name on behalf of all the names entrusted to us, the names of all whose lives have impacted on ours, in the hope that none might be forgotten, none lost; that mercy might extend to all.

From this point of view we better see what it might mean to speak of Christ's breast as an 'ark of broad charity' where there is potentially room for all, if only they would

---

[*] Rev. 21.19–20, 14.
[†] Rev. 21.23.

not decline the invitation to enter. The weak find a firm foundation there. The exhausted find rest. Our own tense breast is enabled to relax, extending in scope to let our lungs breathe fully, oxygenized by great draughts of Spirit.

The one within whose breast this healing transformation takes place is at once Son of God and Son of Mary. As our Maker he is our Judge; as our Bearer he holds us with maternal tenderness. Julian of Norwich once audaciously wrote: 'Jesus Christ who does good in return for evil is our true mother; we have our being from him where the ground of motherhood begins, with all the precious safekeeping of love which endlessly follows.'[*] Christ's breast embodies the high-priestly breastplate, the rampart of the City of God. It is also the repository of God's maternal love.

> Lord Jesus, may I rest upon your breast with a child's
> guilelessness yet with keen attention: never let me
> betray you! Call to mind kindly the names that
> are inextricable from mine. Extend your love to all
> and lead us home together.

---

[*]From chapter 59 of the Long Text of the *Revelations of Divine Love*, trans. Barry Windeatt (London: Folio Society, 2017), p. 197.

Ad cor – To the Heart

Summi Regis cor, aveto,
Te saluto corde laeto,
Te complecti me delectat,
Et hoc meum cor affectat,
   Ut ad te loquar, animes.

Quo amore vincebaris,
Quo dolore torquebaris,
Cum te totum exhaurires,
Ut te nobis impartires,
   Et nos a morte tolleres?

O mors illa quam amara,
Quam immitis, quam avara;
Quae per cellam introivit,
In qua mundi vita vivit,
   Te mordens, cor dulcissimum!

Propter mortem quam tulisti
Quando pro me defecisti,
Cordis mei cor dilectum,
In te meum fer affectum,
   Hoc est quod opto plurimum.

O cor dulce praedilectum,
Munda cor meum illectum,
Et in vanis induratum;
Pium fac et timoratum,
   Repulso tetro frigore.

AD COR – TO THE HEART

Hail, heart of the highest King,
with a glad heart I salute you.
To encompass you delights me;
it moves my heart.
Stir me up to speak to you!

Who can say how lovingly you conquered,
how painfully you were racked
when you poured yourself out fully
to give yourself to us
and to carry us away from death.

How bitter that death was
when proud and avaricious
it entered the cell in which
the life of the world was alive;
there it bit you, sweetest heart.

By the death you bore when
you fainted for my sake,
beloved heart of my heart,
draw to yourself my affection:
this is what I wish for most of all.

O sweet, most beloved heart,
purify my heart that has been tricked,
hardened by vanities;
make it faithful and God-fearing:
drive its dreadful coldness away.

Per medullam cordis mei,
Peccatoris atque rei,
Tuus amor transferatur,
Quo cor totum rapiatur
   Languens amoris vulnere.

Dilatare, aperire,
Tanquam rosa fragrans mire,
Cordi meo te conjunge,
Unge illud et compunge;
   Qui amat te, quid patitur?

Quidnam agat nescit vere,
Nec se valet cohibere,
Nullum modum dat amori,
Multa morte vellet mori,
   Amore quisquis vincitur.

Viva cordis voce clamo,
Dulce cor; te namque amo:
Ad cor meum inclinare,
Ut se possit applicare,
   Devoto tibi pectore.

Tuo vivat in amore
Ne dormitet in torpore,
Ad te oret, ad te ploret
Te adoret, te honoret,
   Te fruens omni tempore.

Rosa cordis, aperire,
Cujus odor fragrat mire,
Te dignare dilatare,
Fac cor meum anhelare
   Flamma desiderii.

AD COR — TO THE HEART

I am a sinner and a guilty man:
let your love pass
through my heart of hearts,
that my whole heart may be ravished
and languish with a wound of love.

Open up and broaden
like a wonderfully fragrant rose;
bind yourself to my heart.
Anoint it, let it know compunction.
What will one who loves you suffer?

Whoever is conquered by love
is at pains to know how to act:
he cannot restrain himself;
his love knows no measure.
He is ready to die many deaths.

With my heart's full voice I cry,
sweet heart, for I love you.
Bend down towards my heart,
that it may join itself to you,
from within a devoted breast.

May it live in love of you,
let it not sluggishly slumber.
May it pray and weep before you,
adore you and honour you,
in constant enjoyment of you.

Christ's heart's red rose, open up!
Spread your wondrous fragrance.
Be pleased to broaden,
and let my heart strain forward
aflame with desire.

Da cor cordi sociari,
Tecum, Jesu, vulnerari.
Nam [cor] cordi similatur,
Si cor meum perforatur
   Sagittis improperii.

Infer tuum intra sinum
Cor ut tibi sit vicinum,
In dolore gaudioso
Cum deformi specioso,
   Quod vix se ipsum capiat.

Hic repauset, hic moretur,
Ecce jam post te movetur,
Te ardenter vult sitire.
Jesu, noli contraire,
   Ut bene de te sentiat.

AD COR – TO THE HEART

Let my heart be joined to yours and be
wounded, Jesus, in communion with you.
For my heart resembles your heart
when it is pierced
by arrows of reproach.

Let my heart enter your intimacy,
that it may be near you
in joy-filled grief, united with
the beautiful one who was disfigured,
so that it can hardly comprehend itself.

In this state may it rest and remain.
See, it moves towards you already,
ardently wishing to thirst for you.
Jesus, do not turn away from it!
Let it know your benevolence.

Years ago a friend who is an artist received a commission to decorate a chapel to the Sacred Heart of Jesus. After initial exchanges with the commissioners she rang me in distress and said, 'I *cannot* draw a gingerbread heart!'

The aesthetic code attaching to Sacred Heart devotions makes this theological symbol dear and familiar to many. Others feel estranged by it, even repulsed.

The 'gingerbread heart', a schematic, often thorn-crowned, flame-emitting heart-shape shown on its own, on the Saviour's open breast, or held in his hand, has been divulged on devotional cards and in prayer books, in statuary, paintings and mosaics for centuries. The motif is popular and well-loved to this day. It has become something of a brand mark of Catholicism.

We may dismiss expressions of it as kitsch, and we should be right, perhaps. But religious kitsch may at times deserve our respect, albeit grudging. If a given image exercises broad appeal over time and across cultural boundaries; if it provokes the noblest sentiments of people of good will, something about it touches intelligent and venerable depths even if its outward form seems superficial.

The novelist Martin Mosebach has written perceptively about this phenomenon in a fine essay, 'In Praise of the Lourdes Madonna'. He speaks of the aesthetic outrage one might feel on seeing an unsubtle, serialized devotional object installed in a baroque or Gothic interior, plonked within a makeshift shrine, but goes on to observe that the faithful more often than not do not feel any awkwardness. They flock to these undistinguished corners of ancient churches to light candles, then go on to bring the image out of church, into their homes.

Mosebach first set eyes on the Lourdes Madonna when he was a child. He found her enthroned on the bedroom dresser of a couple of stout Rheingau winegrowers. Their little daughter showed him round the whole house while his parents were downstairs sipping samples. He was enchanted. Later he found her again and again in diverse settings: 'At her feet, in convent corridors, one could find a half-dried African violet and a grateful cactus, yet her true home was an artificial grotto,' by preference in pumice, 'like the landscaping for a miniature electric train'.

> Lourdes grottoes abounded, not just in the Vatican alongside Renaissance *palazzetti*, but also in the heart of dangerous, violent metropolises: in Cairo and New York, in Seoul and Bogotà . . . ; the grotto was also a natural collage for the walls of huge apartment blocks. In front of these caves were always a couple of people; red carnations in cellophane bags hung on the railings.[*]

To bookish, art-loving people creations such as these are an embarrassment. They are dismissed precisely because they are kitsch, instances of mass-produced, poor-quality replication that signals the demise of decent craft. Mass production, though, presupposes a mass market; it corresponds to a sensibility widely shared. The universality of a design that, defying the passing of fashions, endures unperturbed, placidly itself, unconcerned to impress,

---

[*] Martin Mosebach, *Subversive Catholicism: Papacy, Liturgy, Church*, trans. Sebastian Condon and Graham Harrison (Brooklyn, NY: Angelico Press, 2019), p. 142f.

should make us consider whether it may not, in fact, be the shrewd, delicate keeper of a great mystery.

Cordelia Spaemann once told Mosebach that the devotional kitsch of places of pilgrimage is 'the protective wall that keeps the smug aesthetes – she called them the "pack of aesthetes" – away from the sanctuary', maintaining the holy place as the precinct of the poor and pure of heart who, in the optic of the Beatitudes, are the true seers of this ages and heirs to heaven's kingdom.[*]

Mosebach's reflections on the Lourdes Madonna apply just as much to the Sacred Heart. Indeed, the two will often appear as a pair of non-identical twins displayed side by side in parallel niches, at once founts of benediction and guardians of the temple, gently accusing the sophistication of passers-by who shudder at their ordinariness while others are touched and bring these objects into their lives. Paul Selmer, the young hero of Sigrid Undset's conversion novel *The Wild Orchid*, is at first appalled by the 'house gods' he finds on display in the jejune home of a Catholic family providing him with digs in Oslo sometime in the 1920s. He is also fascinated: 'Above the sofa between the windows hung a colossal oleograph of Jesus pointing towards his heart, which he had arranged outside his clothes and out of which flames burst forth through a little chimney.'[†] It is noteworthy that Undset, like Mosebach, associates this kind of popular devotion with industry or the steam train, that

---

[*] Ibid., p. 145, cf. Mt. 5.3, 8.
[†] The description occurs in chapter three of Part One of *The Wild Orchid*, first published in Oslo by Aschehoug in 1929 under the title *Gymnadenia*.

most democratic of conveyances, as if to suggest that here there is space for all, that here is an engine of spirituality that will keep you on track.

And is it not fitting, in fact, that the Sacred Heart, which in the symbolic order expresses the realism of God's incarnation, *should* stand before us as nothing at all special, like the train that takes you to work? As such it is a likeness of our lives, which most of the time, let us face it, tend to be 'obscure, laborious, and ordinary'.*

To understand the significance of the Sacred Heart in theology, and in the prayer of the faithful, we must remember that it is at once concrete and symbolic. As the animating principle of embodied existence Jesus's human heart had all the physical reality of our hearts, yours and mine, subject to emotions and fatigue, well-being and malaise. The heart is fundamentally the guarantor of life. When Jesus breathed his last, his heart stopped; his pulse fainted. When he was carried to his tomb, bewailed by heartbroken myrrh-bearers, his heart of flesh was to all intents and purposes simply that, flesh and nothing else.

Yet his divine nature was untouched by death's claws, his uncreated 'heart' not missing a beat. We are back to the tension I addressed in the first chapter. We need words and

---

*A phrase from the Constitutions of the Order of Cistercians of the Strict Observance. It occurs in a passage, Cst. 3.5, which stresses that only by preferring nothing to Christ will the monks 'be happy to persevere in a life that is ordinary, obscure, and laborious'. By describing monastic life in these terms, the Order simply stresses that it is a *human* life.

terms, images and a prayerful logic apt to keep passion and impassibility, death and indestructible life together.

The councils provided all this in their austere deliberations, hard of access. It may help to adduce an example from life. After all, this theological balancing act touches each believer personally as a confessional imperative.

In a text from the early 1980s, Dame Felicitas Corrigan, a Benedictine of Stanbrook, reflected on a passage from the *Revelations* of Julian of Norwich. In chapter 4 of the *Long Text*, Julian, full of grief, contemplates the passion of Jesus. She is then suddenly astounded to find her heart filled with joy. In the middle of the passion scene she entertains a revelation of the Blessed Trinity. The two realities of human dereliction and divine fullness are inseparable, she discovers, and only by keeping them together, 'his blessed Passion along with the Godhead', will she find strength and grace to confront any trial.[*] Dame Felicitas cites this expostulation of a medieval witness, then illustrates it by means of a private recollection from her monastic novitiate just ahead of the Second World War.

One day, she writes, she noticed that her novice mistress, Dame Joanna Hopkins, 'a contemplative of the first rank', was in spiritual distress. She sensed that something essential was going on, so mustered courage to knock on the older nun's cell door. She found her 'sitting in tears, an open breviary on her lap', declaring curtly that she was saying her office and did not wish to be disturbed. The novice noticed that the book was not open at the office for the day, but at a

---

[*] From chapter 4 of the Long Text of the *Revelations of Divine Love*, p. 62f.

AD COR – TO THE HEART

page that displayed Psalm 22, the great Passion Psalm: 'My God, my God, why have you forsaken me?' She pointed this out to Dame Joanna. 'At this, all annoyance vanished, and she replied: "To think that all during the Passion, there was not a ripple over the surface of the Blessed Trinity."'[*] Only in the light of this perception will we begin to see the full range of salvific sense to be found in the Sacred Heart of Jesus. Our own heart, like that of the contemplative nun, must be pierced by the paradox.

Scripture does not wait until the announcement of the incarnation to speak of God's heart. In fact, the image first occurs early in Genesis, in a passage telling of the earthly consequence of man's fall from grace:

> The Lord saw that the wickedness of man was great in the earth, and that every imagination of the thoughts of his heart was only evil continually. And the Lord was sorry that he had made man on the earth, and it grieved him to his heart.[†]

There is pathos in this utterance. It indicates for the first time divine vulnerability. God is eternal, yes, and beyond the vicissitudes of earthly fortune and misfortune; yet such is the bond between him and the human being fashioned in his image that this creature of dust is able to wound him,

---

[*] This text, 'What Christ Means to Me', is published in Dame Felicitas Corrigan's anthology *Benedictine Tapestry* (London: Darton, Longman and Todd, 1991), p. 106.
[†] Gen. 6.5–6.

producing an anguish that makes it seem as if God has a heart like man's.

This terminology makes no sense strictly speaking. God has no physiognomy. To speak of God's 'heart' is mere approximation through an excess of language; but it is a telling approximation. Even as God has left his mark upon man, it is as though man had left his mark upon God. We get an idea of the intensity of this relationship when, later, through Isaiah, the Lord exclaims: 'Can a woman forget her nursing child, or show no compassion for the child of her womb?'[*] Compassion is the apposite word, to be construed in its most radical sense as a suffering-with.

We touch, here, on a sublime aspect of Judaeo–Christian faith: the conviction that God has so engaged himself in the story of humanity that he feels our drama as his, and is somehow internal to it from creation on. The connection is rendered concrete in the incarnation, whose point of supreme intensity is Christ's heart. To fix our attention on it is to consider God's personal passion, as ancient as time, for our sake.

In his Letter to the Romans, at the end of the grand eighth chapter which outlines the terms of new life in the Spirit, Paul states this certainty: 'I am sure that neither death, nor life, nor angels, nor principalities, nor things present, nor things to come, nor powers, nor height, nor depth, nor anything else in all creation, will be able to separate us from the love of God in Christ Jesus our Lord.'[†] I dare say we are

---

[*] Isa. 49.15.
[†] Rom. 8.38f.

AD COR – TO THE HEART

used to reading this passage as reassurance to ourselves. No circumstance, we reflect, is so awful that I cannot at any point extend my hand and grasp God's, which protects me. This mindset is not mistaken, but it is imperfect. It lacks solidity, like the milky food of infants.[*] It resembles a child's prayer at bedtime, as in Engelbert Humperdinck's *Hansel and Gretel*, where a brother and sister, lost in the woods at night, pray in words composed by Humperdinck's own sister Adelheid:

> When at night I go to sleep,
> Fourteen angels watch do keep,
> Two my head are guarding,
> Two my feet are guiding;
> Two upon my right hand,
> Two upon my left hand.
> Two who warmly cover,
> Two who o'er me hover,
> Two to whom 'tis given
> To guide my steps to heaven.[†]

Humperdinck set this text to alluring harmonies. There is sweetness in the prayer's sentiment. But the children are not, in fact, safe. The prayer is preceded by the appearance of the ambiguous Sandman, who blurs the children's sense of the real. The interlude following the prayer is called

---

[*] Cf. 1 Cor. 3.1–3; 1 Pet. 2.2.

[†] This unattributed version is from the Rullman bilingual libretto published in New York in 1905 for performances on Broadway.

'Dream Pantomime', as if the invocation of angels were mere performance. Close by is the cottage of the Gingerbread Witch, who waits to devour Hansel and Gretel, a fairy-tale symbol of whatever peril haunts us. To confront such peril in peace, without panic, more is needed than the mere form of a gingerbread heart and a beguiling song.

To live is at times to suffer. When Paul affirms that Christ's love is inseparable from us, it is not by means of a promise that we shall be kept invulnerable; rather he tells us that pain can be illumined and despair dispelled by Jesus's love. If we make of that love our dwelling place and constant criterion of judgement, speech and action, it will envelop us like a coat of arms whose parts articulate virtues flowing from love: truth, righteousness, peace and faith. On our head will be the helmet of salvation. Our hands will wield the Spirit's sword. Our feet will bear us wherever we must go to proclaim the Gospel of peace. We shall not be beyond the reach of the 'wiles of the evil one', but we shall be equipped to withstand them.[*] That is what matters. To know the love alive in Christ's heart is to stand unflinching in trial and thereby to discover in our weakness a strength not our own.[†]

The Sacred Heart of Jesus provides for this reality of battle *and* communion a spatial imagery that complements the metaphors of armour. The heart is supremely sensitive. At the same time it is unbelievably robust. Anyone who has sat at a deathbed, observing the heart's faithfully ongoing thump

---

[*] Eph. 6.10–17.
[†] 2 Cor. 12.9.

when the rest of the physical organism has shut down, will have been awed by this fact. The heart of Jesus is an environment within which we can confront life's hardship without need for recourse to pious wishful thinking. We can face whatever it is *as* it is, open-eyed, and yet not be overwhelmed, contained by and united with this invincible engine of salvific life and strength, inexhaustibly compassionate in its humanity, in its divinity a source of incomprehensible peace. The Sacred Heart lets us own the human condition, even at its most imperilled, within a *milieu divin*.

The Sacred Heart's potential as a symbol of Christian realism is implicit, as we have seen, in Scripture, yet lay largely dormant for a thousand years or so, like a seed waiting for a fair day and favourable sunshine. It is no coincidence that Sacred Heart devotion flourished within and was shaped by the Cistercian movement that started with the founding of Cistercium, or Cîteaux, in 1098. For the early Cistercians were realists at every level, keen to embody high ideals. Pauline Matarasso has written of St Stephen Harding, third abbot of Cîteaux, that everything he touched 'bears witness to his pursuit of authenticity, of the spirit that only the authentic letter can set free'.[*] Abbot Stephen and his brethren knew that appeals to the spirit alone lead easily to abstraction and lived compromise: the spirit calls for being spelled out, and fleshed out.

Even as the Word was made flesh, the Christian's spiritual quest engages our physicality. Much of what has

---

[*] *The Cistercian World: Monastic Writings from the Twelfth Century*, trans. and ed. Pauline Matarasso (London: Penguin, 1993), p. 10.

been described as gloomy Cistercian 'strict observance' – the vigils and fasting, the Passion devotions, the ample liturgical gestures, the tangibility of death, with bodies at funerals laid out on a plank, without a coffin – is not, in fact, primarily to do with mortification but with resolve to keep the body engaged in the spirit's pursuits. Once this point is grasped, the lugubrious mythology of Cîteaux evaporates like morning mist and one discovers, with the rising of the sun, the Order's joyfulness and intrinsic lightness of step.

Conscious of their own human nature in all its dimensions, the Cistercians were devoted to Christ's humanity. St Bernard was exemplary in this regard. He scrutinized the life of Jesus from conception to death. He was one of the first Christian writers to explicitly thematize the Sacred Heart, notably in a sermon on the Song of Songs, which develops the Song's image of the 'cleft of the rock', a place in which Lover and Beloved meet in mystic communion. Bernard finds, as we saw above, considering the section *Ad latus*, in this image a manner of speaking of Christ's wounds.

He imagines Longinus's spear as a probe letting us glimpse the fount of Christ's love from within. His turn of phrase is wonderfully compact: '*Patet arcanum cordis per foramina corporis; patet magnum illud pietatis sacramentum; patent viscera misericordiae Dei nostri, in quibus visitavit nos oriens ex alto.*' By means of this threefold *pate(n)t*, affirmations of evidence, Christ's heart is envisaged first as *arcanum*, a word that indicates both secret knowledge and a secret place. The Sacred Heart is a source of revelation and a space within which we can subsist, made accessible '*per foramina corporis*', 'by means of the body's perforation'.

AD COR – TO THE HEART

It is next a 'great sacrament of piety', *pietas* having the resonance of determined fidelity. The third qualification draws on the *Benedictus*, the New Testament canticle sung daily in the Church's liturgy at Lauds. Luke tells us that Zachary proclaimed it in a kind of ecstasy at the naming of his son John, Christ's Forerunner. Reference to the patent 'loving-kindness of the heart of our God, who visits us like the dawn from on high' pertains to the Messiah's imminent birth. By the simplest of rhetorical means, straightforward juxtaposition, Bernard links Christ's passion on Calvary to his birth of Mary, regarding both epiphanies as revelations of the Father's loving heart.*

If you read Bernard's sermon in full you will see why the *Rhythmica oratio* was long attributed to him. The accents are the same. The *oratio* is like a metrical elevation of the sermon's prose. Arnulf of Leuven is sure to have known Bernard's text. By the time he was elected abbot of Villers the *Sermons on the Song of Songs* had become a canonical reference in the Order. The connaturality of his sensibility and Bernard's shows that the unanimity for which the Cistercians strove was expressed not only in timetables, rubrics and architecture, but also in a shared approach to the salvific mystery.

Arnulf is only one of many thirteenth-century Cistercian voices that take Bernard's intuitions further, drawing out of them implicit harmonies, quite the way Cistercian

---

*An excerpt from St Bernard's sixty-first sermon on the Song of Songs is given in the Catholic Breviary's Office of Readings on Wednesday in the third week of ordinary time. The reference to the 'clefts to the rock' can be found in the Song of Songs 2.14; the verse from the *Benedictus* in Lk. 1.78.

churches of the time were fitted with resonating chambers to extend the acoustic, producing subtle polyphonies from monody.

It is well known that the theology of the Sacred Heart was decisively developed in the German abbey of Helfta, whose formidable nuns put paid to stereotypes of medieval women as universally cowed. Gertrude of Helfta, alongside two sisters both called Mechtilde, laid the doctrinal foundation that let Sacred Heart devotions spread throughout Western Christendom. The lives of all three overlapped with Arnulf's. Their contributions to theology are substantial.

The mysticism of the Sacred Heart does not presuppose, however, an intellectual temperament. That is why I would say that an even more characteristic contemporary Cistercian witness is St Lutgarde of Aywières, who died in 1246.

Lutgarde's biographer, the Dominican Thomas of Cantimpré, who had been a student of Albert the Great, tells us how this stalwart nun grew in grace of discipleship through identifiable stages: by mortification and prayer her hardness of heart was dispelled; she felt compassion for the suffering; her compassion led her into a deeper understanding of Scripture. Her heart, though, longed for more than good deeds and the illumination of her mind. It longed to beat with the rhythm of Christ's own heart, and to be filled with that heart's love.

She made it known to Jesus that she had an audacious wish. 'What would you like?' he asked. 'Your heart, Lord,' she said, only to be told: 'And I want yours.' Lutgarde consented: 'Let it be so, Lord, but in such a way that you temper the love of your heart to my heart, and I possess my heart in you, to be ever secure in your protection.' Thanks to this exchange of hearts, Lutgarde lived for the rest of her life in existential awareness of what it means to love as Jesus loves.[*]

The intensity of that experience is inconceivable for most of us. Lutgarde knew the anguish of Christ's heart; she also knew its exultant peace. She lived within a vast span of compassion and adoration. She became blind. But it was as if the loss of physical vision illumined her inner eye. She was given the charism of reading others' hearts, of working healings; she became a bearer of consolation to countless people. Her example may seem remote, perhaps extreme, yet is neither. Any baptized Christian is called to know the heart of Jesus from within. I love the old Latin prayer, '*Iesu, mitis et humilis Corde, fac cor nostrum secundum Cor tuum*': 'Jesus, meek and humble of heart, make our hearts like your heart.' This intention is the theme on which Arnulf improvises, pointing towards participation in Christ's redeeming work: 'What will one who loves you suffer?'

In John's Gospel, the mutual indwelling of the believer and Christ is expounded in eucharistic terms: 'He who eats my flesh and drinks my blood abides in me, and I in him.'[†] Holy communion is an exchange of hearts, possibly in more palpable terms than we commonly realize. It is intriguing that in the case of alleged eucharistic miracles the changed specimens, submitted to scientific analysis, almost

---

[*]*Vita Sanctae Lutgardis* I.12. A convenient bilingual online edition of this text was published by Mark Reynolds in 2023. It can be found on www.archive.org.
[†]Jn 6.56.

invariably show traces of cardiac tissue.* Such miracles are not truths of the faith: no-one is obliged to acknowledge them. But anyone can find here a telling symbol.

Christ's body, given for us, is in a privileged manner his heart, burning with love for humankind, bursting with grief on account of man's scornful rejection of this love. Through this heart, our hearts are given what they need to unfold and to reveal, as Arnulf would say, 'like a rose', their fragrance, form and loveliness.

> Lord Jesus, prepare my heart, by whatever means it takes,
> to resemble yours. Let me follow you in good heart,
> contrite and jubilant at once, tasting your freedom.
> My heart, Lord, is at your disposal. Broaden it to
> become for you a hospitable home.

---

*See for instance Franco Serafini, *A Cardiologist Examines Jesus* (Manchester, NH: Sophia Institute Press, 2021).

Ad faciem – To the Face

Salve, caput cruentatum,
Totum spinis coronatum,
Conquassatum, vulneratum,
Arundine verberatum,
   Facie sputis illita.

Salve, cujus dulcis vultus,
Immutatus et incultus,
Immutavit suum florem,
Totus versus in pallorem
   Quem [cupit] coeli curia.

Omnis vigor atque viror
Hinc recessit, non admiror,
Mors apparet in aspectu
Totus pendens in defectu,
   Attritus aegra macie.

Sic affectus, sic despectus,
Propter me sic interfectus,
Peccatori tam indigno
Cum amoris intersigno
   Appare clara facie.

In hac tua passione,
Me agnosce, Pastor bone,
Cujus sumpsi mel ex ore,
Haustum lactis cum dulcore,
   Prae omnibus deliciis.

AD FACIEM – TO THE FACE

Hail, blood-stained head,
crowned all round with thorns,
crushed and wounded,
beaten with a rod,
your face besmeared with spittle.

Your sweet countenance is
changed and untended.
Its flower is discoloured,
turned entirely to pallor,
yet desired by the heavenly host.

Your vigour and green freshness
have receded; I see nothing to admire.
Death appears in your aspect
as you hang there undone,
worn out by emaciated pain.

Thus affected and despised,
reduced to nothing for my sake:
show me, an unworthy sinner,
your face's radiance,
holding up the banner of your love.

Recognize me in this passion of yours,
good shepherd,
from whose mouth I harvest honey
drawn with the sweetness of milk,
surpassing all other delights.

Non me reum asperneris,
Nec indignum dedigneris,
Morte tibi jam vicina,
Tuum caput hic inclina,
  In meis pausa brachiis.

Tuae sanctae passioni
Me gauderem interponi,
In hac cruce tecum mori:
Praesta crucis amatori,
  Sub cruce tua moriar.

Morti tuae tam [amarae]
Grates ago, Jesu chare;
Qui es clemens, pie Deus,
Fac quod petit tuus reus,
  Ut absque te non finiar.

Dum me mori est necesse,
Noli mihi tunc deesse;
In tremenda mortis hora
Veni, Jesu, absque mora,
  Tuere me et libera.

Cum me jubes emigrare,
Jesu chare, tunc appare:
O amator amplectende,
Temetipsum tunc ostende
  In cruce salutifera.

AD FACIEM — TO THE FACE

Do not spurn me, the guilty one.
Do not reject me, the unworthy.
With your death at hand,
lean your head towards me
and rest in my embrace.

In your sacred passion
I would gladly have a part
to suffer death on this cross with you.
Let one who loves the cross
face death underneath your cross.

To your bitter death
I give thanks, dear Jesus.
Faithful God, how good you are!
Grant what your guilty one asks:
let me not end up far from you.

One day I will have to die.
Be not absent from me then!
In death's tremendous hour,
Jesus, come without delay
to protect and free me.

When you bid me leave the land
of the living, dear Jesus, appear!
You are loving; I would hold you tight.
Show yourself to me then,
on your cross, the fount of healing.

A cry repeatedly, passionately uttered in the Psalms, the Church's great prayer book, is this: 'Your face, Lord, I seek. Hide not your face from me.' The Lord's face is perceived as shining. To be deprived of its light is to be cast off 'like those who go down to the Pit'. To behold it is to be comforted, wrapt in mercy and truth.[*]

It is said of Moses, whose countenance shone with reflected glory, that he spoke to the Lord 'face to face'.[†] We are instantly reminded, though, that this is a figure of speech. Already Jacob had taken it for granted that no mortal can see God and live. The object of his vision at Peniel was a nocturnal messenger of glory, not the radiant Godhead.[‡] When Moses, with the chutzpah of earth's humblest man, asked to see God's substantial glory, the Lord retorted:

> 'I will make all my goodness pass before you, and will proclaim before you my name "The Lord"; and I will be gracious to whom I will be gracious, and will show mercy on whom I will show mercy. But', he said, 'you cannot see my face; for man shall not see me and live.' And the Lord said, 'Behold, there is a place by me where you shall stand upon the rock; and while my glory passes by I will put you in a cleft of the rock, and I will cover you with my hand until I have passed by; then I will take away my hand, and you shall see my back; but my face shall not be seen.'[§]

---

[*] Psalm 27.8f., 80.7, 88.14, 143.7, 89.14.
[†] Exod. 33.11.
[‡] Gen. 32.30. Cf. the vision of Manoah and his wife in Judg. 13.
[§] Exod. 33.19–23; cf. Num. 12.3.

This oracle originates the image of the rock-cleft we have already considered in the posterior context of the Song of Songs. Only by retreating into the solidest form of matter can human nature endure the momentary passage of immaterial splendour.

Our sight is not equipped to look upon divinity; our natural being cannot endure it. The discomfort we feel and the risks we run when we try to gaze upon the sun, be it in eclipse, are merely a parable of the discrepancy between our seeing, our being and uncreated Light. Even the most virtuous of men could only bear to see God's 'back', and that, from a distance. Similar qualifications are made regarding the theophanies of which Isaiah and Ezekiel speak, the latter stressing that the most human eyes can perceive in an encounter with the Holy One is 'the appearance of the likeness of the glory of the Lord'.[*]

It pertains to the wonder of the incarnation that this perennial non-seeing yields to vision. Being, in the words of the Nicene Creed, 'God from God, Light from Light', Jesus reveals the face of God in human features. When the Blessed Virgin, having given birth, looked into this face, she enjoyed a privilege no woman or man had known since Adam and Eve before the fall, still robed in glory. Sin subsequently darkened their vision, making God alien, blinding humankind to divine realities. When Christ was born, light again poured out on the world: the people who sat in darkness saw a great

---

[*] Isa. 6.1–5; Ezek. 1.26–8.

light.[*] A categorically new way of seeing was enabled. In a catechetical poem St Ephrem the Syrian explains amiably:

> The world, you see, had two eyes fixed in it:
> Eve was its left eye, blind,
> While the right eye, illumined, is Mary.
>
> Through the darkened eye the whole world was dark;
> People groped and thought each stone they stumbled
> On was god, calling falsehood truth.
>
> Illumined by the other eye and by heaven's Light
> Residing in its midst, humanity was reconciled again.
> It saw that its discovery had ruined its life.[†]

Deprived through sin's corruption of ability to look on God, human beings lacked criteria by which to distinguish between earthly and transcendent things. They fell into the trap of idolizing *stuff*. Restored by grace to sight, they realized that the fruit of transgression, temptingly advertised as gain, had turned out to be a fatal loss. Life and light were restored to them as gifts. The overwhelming beauty of God's face, revealed as that of an infant so as not to make them afraid, drew forth afresh the image of God that lay hidden in themselves, in large measure forgotten.

---

[*] Cf. Mt. 4.16, citing Isa. 9.2.
[†] Ephrem the Syrian, *Select Poems*, trans. Sebastian P. Brock and George A. Kiraz (Provo, Utah: Brigham Young University Press, 2006), p. 67. I have contracted and somewhat altered the translation, which in this bilingual edition is provided primarily as a crib to the Syriac text, in order to stay closer to St Ephrem's crisp style.

AD FACIEM — TO THE FACE

What the fulfilment of Israel's remnant's millennial longing – 'Show me, Lord, your face!' – may have looked like is suggested by certain visionary artists. I think of the Nativity scene in Giotto's wonderful Life of Christ cycle in the Scrovegni Chapel in Padua. We see the Virgin mesmerized by the face of her Child, who looks back into her eyes probingly. In this silent exchange God's cry to humanity in Eden, 'Where are you?' is answered at last: We are here. The Virgin's posture turns, on our behalf, an ancient No into a Yes; where Eve had hidden, Mary is exposed, facing God; mankind's imbecile urge to flee is transformed, in her, into will to remain, never to lose sight of this face supremely loved, even when she sees it contorted with pain inflicted by Adam's still unseeing children.

The Gospels let us catch fugitive glimpses of what people saw in Jesus's face. When, early in his public ministry, he asked an assembly gathered for worship in the synagogue whether it is lawful 'to do good or to do harm on the Sabbath, to save life or to kill', all stayed silent, looking down. He looked at them with anger, then, grieved at their hardness of heart.[*] We are salutarily reminded that God's face is not always smiling with a father's indulgence at his children's charming play. After all, we are not to stay children. We are to grow up, to consider our call and assume responsibility for it, mindful that we have work to do and that God's Son, ever at work, like his Father, expects us to do it well, one in him, in the strength of the Spirit.[†] We shall be called to

---

[*] Mk 3.1–5.
[†] 1 Cor. 1.26; Jn 5.17; Eph. 3.16.

account both for what we have done and for what we have failed to do.* Belief in God's mercy does not blot out the biblical reality of God's dispassionate wrath, which is the engagement of his justice with our villainy.

Encountering fidelity and good will, Jesus's face, forbidding in majesty, displays beneficial affirmation. Surrounded by an intently listening crowd, he looks around and says: 'Here are my mother and my brothers! Whoever does the will of God is my brother and sister and mother.' This is not to cancel the bonds of flesh that tie him to his physical family, but to ascertain that anyone who stays close to him, 'walking as he walked', can reach that same level of intimacy.†

And who can imagine what that young man must have felt who, coming up to Jesus to ask how he might inherit life eternal, found Jesus looking at him with great love, saying, 'You lack one thing,' that thing being the surrender of all in which, until that moment, he had put his trust.

To encounter the radiance of God's face in Christ is sweet. It is also risky. Coming to him guilty, in hope of forgiveness, I cannot separate his pardon from his clear summons: 'From now on sin no more.'‡ The question is: do I seek the face of God only in distress, when more manageable supports let me down, or do I desire to live before it constantly?

The enchantment exercised by Jesus's face is evidenced by an old tradition concerning Abgar, King of Edessa.

---

*Mt. 25.31ff.
†Mk 3.31–5; cf. 1 Jn 2.6.
‡Mk 10.17–22; Jn 8.11.

Eusebius relates it in the first part of his *Church History*, datable to the third century. Abgar was a contemporary of Jesus's. Eusebius describes him as 'the brilliantly successful monarch of the peoples of Mesopotamia'. Abgar's delight in his accomplishments was tempered by chronic illness. Having heard of the cures Jesus worked in Palestine, Abgar hoped he, too, might be healed. He wrote Jesus a letter, asking him to visit. Eusebius says he found a copy of it in Edessa's Record Office, then translated it word for word from Syriac. It is a gracious invitation. Abgar tells of what he has heard of Jesus's signs; states the conclusion he has drawn – 'either you are God and came down from heaven to do these things, or you are God's Son doing them'; begs him to come to him 'whatever the inconvenience'; then adds that he knows about the opposition Jesus faces and offers him a new base: 'my city is very small, but highly esteemed, adequate for both of us.'

Having cited Abgar's letter, Eusebius copies out Jesus's response, also from the Record Office, one presumes. It proclaims beatitude on the king: 'Blessed are you who have believed in me without having seen me.'[*] Jesus kindly asks to be excused – 'I must complete all that I was sent to do here' – but promises to send, once taken up 'to the One who sent me', one of his disciples to cure Abgar's illness. This promise was fulfilled when Thaddaeus, one of the Seventy, came to Edessa and laid the foundation of that

---

[*] Cf. Jn 21.29.

city's glorious history as an early capital of Christian virtue, mission, doctrine and poetry.*

Eusebius omits a detail of this story which is contained in a roughly contemporary source, a Syriac treatise known as the *Doctrine of Addai*. According to it, the messenger sent by Abgar to carry his letter was not content just to pick up a reply by return of post. Happening to be a painter, 'he took and painted a likeness of Jesus with choice paints, and brought it with him to Abgar the king, his master. And when Abgar the king saw the likeness, he received it with great joy, and placed it with great honour in one of his palatial houses.'† This icon is said to be the origin of the type known as Mandylion, portraying the Saviour's head on an unfurled cloth. Later sources refer to it as *acheiropoieton*, 'not made with hands', positing that Christ's likeness, rather than being painted by an Edessan court official, was imprinted on a towel which the Lord had used to wash and dry his face.

Be that as it may. What matters is that Christ's face, even imperfectly reproduced, was early understood to be *evangelion*, 'good news', in its own right. The Church was wary of reducing the Gospel of Jesus, 'the image [*eikōn*] of the invisible God',‡ to mere precepts, presciently aware of that tedious Christian tendency, denounced later by the Orcadian poet Edwin Muir, to 'unmake' the image,

---

*Eusebius, *The History of the Church from Christ to Constantine,* trans. G. A. Williamson, rev. and ed. Andrew Louth (London: Penguin, 1989), pp. xxxi, 30ff.
†*The Doctrine of Addai, the Apostle,* trans. George Phillips (London: Trübner, 1876), p. 5. Addai is a variant of the name Thaddaeus.
‡Col. 1.15.

AD FACIEM — TO THE FACE

reducing the Word incarnate to nothing but a 'word in flourish and arrogant crook',

> . . . God three angry letters in a book,
> And there the logical hook
> On which the Mystery is impaled and bent
> Into an ideological argument.[*]

The legend of the Holy Face of Edessa accounts for the birth of iconography. It invites us not to forget that the early Church by preference proclaimed the Gospel and offered the Eucharist in a sacred interior overlooked by the *Pantokrator*, the face of Christ looking down on the assembly both as Redeemer and as Judge.

Should we be tempted to regard this visual focus as an aberration seducing us away from the 'purity' of Christ's rational teaching, we might consider an exchange that took place during Jesus's Farewell Discourse after the prophecies of cock-crow and near-universal apostasy.

The apostles, perplexed, try to make sense of the situation's urgency. Thomas, later invited to insert his finger into Christ's wounds, asks aghast, 'Lord, we do not know where you are going – how can we know the way?', only to be told, 'I *am* the way.' Philip then proclaims: 'Lord, show us the Father, and we shall be satisfied.' There is a note of grief in the answer given: 'Have I been with you so long, and

---

[*] The poem 'The Incarnate One' can be found in Edwin Muir, *Collected Poems*, with an introduction by T. S. Eliot (Oxford, New York: Oxford University Press, 1965), p. 228f.

yet you do not know me, Philip? He who has seen me has seen the Father; how can you say, "Show us the Father"?"* The imperative of faith is not only a commandment to hear and obey. A believer must no less learn to see and recognize.

Jesus's assurance that in him, in his face, the Father can be *seen*, that the God who in the Hebrew Bible thunders imprecations at attempts to make of him an image, can yet be represented in embodied form, was a conundrum to the early Church, eager to remain on the right side of orthodoxy and at the same time to take the Word at his word. Gregory of Nyssa, a drawer of subtle distinctions, explains what is at stake in terms of 'image' and 'archetype'. The Father in his unbegottenness is and will ever remain unseeable, he stresses; but part of the purpose of the Son's begetting was to make him known and visible. We see in Jesus a perfect likeness of him in whose bosom the Son *is* from everlasting:[†]

> Just as someone who observes in a pure mirror the reflection of the form that appears there has a vivid knowledge of the face represented, so one who has knowledge of the Son receives in his heart the impress of the Father's hypostasis through his knowledge of the Son. For all that the Father has is discerned in the Son, and all that the Son has is the Father's, because the Son abides wholly in the Father and in turn has the Father wholly in himself. Thus the hypostasis of the Son becomes as it were the form and

---

[*] Jn 14.1–9.
[†] Cf. Jn 1.18.

AD FACIEM — TO THE FACE

face of the knowledge of the Father, and the hypostasis of the Father is known in the form of the Son, while the individuality which is contemplated in them remains as the clear distinction of the hypostases.[*]

The word 'hypostasis' is a term whose root sense is 'foundation' – that which stands or lies underneath. In Gregory's usage, which came to set a standard of orthodoxy, the Persons of the Trinity are conceived of as three hypostases of a single essence (*ousia*). The hypostasis is that about each which permits us to say that there are three; whereas their indivisible essence obliges us to affirm their oneness. Each hypostasis ever presupposes the other two, at once fully itself and pointing beyond itself to trinitarian perfection. In this sense the Son can be said to reveal the Father's face, being its reflection. Whoever looks into the Son's face sees the Father's, too, because the Son 'has the Father wholly in himself'.

The still ongoing elaboration of such theology made the Church of Antiquity cautious in displaying Christ's passion. One was wary of suggesting that the Father, through the Son's pain, had suffered *in Person*. It took a while for trinitarian theology to become fixed and supple enough to embrace the full span of the Word's becoming flesh with adequate equilibration. We are blessed to be heirs to this

---

[*]Gregory of Nyssa, *The Letters*, trans. Anna M. Silvas (Leiden, Boston: Brill, 2007), p. 259. Silvas accounts for the complex reception history of this text, earlier attributed to Gregory's brother, Basil of Caesarea. In her numbering, the reference is to Letter XXXV.8.

heritage of careful definition. At the same time we recognize that Christ's saving passion puts us before a reality that is in the strict sense ineffable. There simply are no words for it. That is why we need texts like Arnulf's: a poetic register able to contain conflicting notions without falling apart in contradiction.

The first couple of stanzas of the section dedicated 'To the Face' evoke realities known to us from the Gospel: the bruises and blood, the spittle, the agonizing thorn-crown. It is recognized that Christ's face, which four of the disciples had seen on Tabor as a source of uncreated light,[*] is 'changed'. Arnulf presupposes the passage from Isaiah traditionally read on Good Friday:

> he had no form or comeliness that we should look at him,
>   and no beauty that we should desire him.
> He was despised and rejected by men;
>   a man of sorrows, and acquainted with grief;
> and as one from whom men hide their faces
>   he was despised, and we esteemed him not.[†]

Yet at the same time he *is* the same, recognizably himself. We tremblingly affirm what John the Evangelist teaches: in and through the cross God's glory erupts as Christ's annihilation manifests a sacrificial love so utter that it subverts and opens up from within the very word 'love', making it at once

---

[*] Mt. 17.2.
[†] Isa. 53.2–3.

AD FACIEM – TO THE FACE

terrible and sweetly comforting. For if love is present *here*, no circumstance is beyond love's reach.

The discoloured flower of Jesus's death-pale face is yet the image of the countenance before which seraphim proclaim their ceaseless cries of 'Holy!' It is 'desired by the heavenly host'. Death, writes Arnulf, appears in Christ's aspect, yet the radiance of Godhead is perceptible. It draws him in, inducing him to stay as close as he can, animated by this firm intention: 'Let me not end up far from you.'

In Eden, when the tragedy of sin entered the world, disrupting its order, man could no longer look upon God's face. He averted his eyes for shame, inadequate now, and sought refuge in matter. When Jesus was born, new vision was enabled. Humanity was gently exercised in sight. We have considered a handful of scenes: in Mary's embrace, in the synagogue, on the road to Jerusalem, on Tabor, in Gethsemane. From these we catch precious glimpses. It is on Mount Calvary, however, that God lays bare his face, letting us examine it in its humiliation at our hands while Jesus's own hands are nailed to the tree, deprived of even the freedom to chase from his face the flies that cannot have been lacking.

Faced with this humbled face we have two options: we can lean back into our certainties, such as they are, and draw a neat line between ourselves and such an unpleasant spectacle, murmuring, 'He saved others, he cannot save himself – let God deliver him now, if he wants to,'[*] then amble home to pour ourselves a drink; or we can meet the defenceless eyes,

---

[*] Cf. Mt. 27.42f.

deeper than the oceans, that look out at us in search of the 'beloved disciple' willing to remain beneath the cross while others run away, willing to know the compassion without which, we are led to see, we shall not have an inkling of who God, Father-Son-and-Spirit, is. The face of Christ crucified calls on me to make a decision that will colour every aspect of my life, from the most public to the secretest. The stance I adopt before it has eternal consequence. I cannot meet the gaze of the *Pantokrator* on his throne if I do not meet them here, on the gibbet, consenting both to see and to be seen.

The most moving passage of the *Rhythmica oratio* occurs in this final section. For a while, we have rather lost the praying subject out of sight. In the first part of the text we saw him grow in stature, rising from prostration to a posture of kneeling to standing on his feet. There he has remained, his attention fixed not so much on himself as on the Beloved fixed before him, probing each aspect of his salvific work, divinely operative in his immobility.

Making Arnulf's words ours, we have prayed for healing, nourishment and pardon. At the end of our meditation, the tables are turned. The poem calls on me to make an act of dispossession. I am asked to abandon fixation on my own misery. What matters now is simply to have eyes for the work Love accomplishes, wishing to support it somehow, desiring to offer some comfort in my turn. Is there anything I can do? Arnulf writes: 'Lean your head towards me/and rest in my embrace.' Can God really need, can he want *my* shoulder to lean on?

I discover the cross as a 'fount of healing' supremely in this: when I break out of my prison of self-centredness, no longer at the mercy of my wounds, but resolved to let my wounds become, united with Christ's through his mystical body, vehicles of mercy, when what my eyes long to see is the Beloved Son's face, and therein a glimmer of the Father's, not my own in a pocket mirror. Seeing myself in him I shall see myself as I truly am. Even my deformities will then be transformed, beautified. I can let my mask fall. The sight of Christ's face will illumine mine.

> Lord Jesus, I long to be seen by you, yet I am afraid. Much in me I do not dare to look at. Reveal your face to me. Let me read there what love means. I wish to know your glory and your grief. May my own face be alive with your kindness.

Flourishing

The *Rhythmica oratio* touched a nerve in contemporary piety. It was widely distributed. Soon it was translated into vernaculars. German-speaking Europe in particular pressed it to its heart. Through a sequence of versions, excerpts were immortalized in Bach's *St Matthew Passion*. The chorale '*O Haupt voll Blut und Wunden*' is a paraphrase of the first stanza of the poem's section '*Ad faciem*'.[*] The Latin version, too, was passed down and cherished. Dietrich Buxtehude, Bach's older contemporary, set a shortened version interspersed with biblical quotations in his exquisite cantata cycle *Membra Iesu Nostri* from 1680. It was through Buxtehude's music that I discovered the poem. This gradual fecundity across linguistic and confessional boundaries is symptomatic of a theme intrinsic to the text itself.[†]

At various points, Abbot Arnulf uses botanic imagery to convey a conviction: in and through its pain, Jesus's passion is productive. It generates life, to be passed on and spread. The glory which the cross embodies in biblical terms is represented poetically in images of flourishing. Arnulf compares the Saviour's wounds to roses unfolding, sprung

---

[*] See Marlies Lehnertz, 'Vom hochmittelalterlichen katholischen Hymnus zum barocken evangelischen Kirchenlied', in *Liturgie und Dichtung: Ein interdisziplinäres Kompendium*, ed. Hansjakob Becker and Reiner Kaczynski (St. Ottilien: EOS, 1983), pp. 755–73.

[†] The transmission history of the *Rhythmica oratio* awaits definitive study. Meanwhile an online essay by Chris Fenner and Dick Wursten written for the Hymnology Archive is invaluable. It can be found at <www.hymnologyarchive.com/salve-mundi-salutare>.

from the cross-stem's branches. Jesus's body, one with the cross, is said to have lost its 'green freshness', but only for the wintry season of his agony and death. Easter Morning will inaugurate a spring that has no end.

This imagery was well established by the thirteenth century. We have looked at the poetry of Venantius Fortunatus, rich in vegetal symbolism. The Passiontide hymn from which I quoted above was sung throughout Europe when Arnulf wrote, drawing on a typology dear to the Fathers of the Church, who saw in Calvary's tree a correspondence to that of Eden. While the tree of which Adam and Eve ate brought death, the cross bears the fruit of life eternal. That fruit is held out to us still in sacramental form. The primordial prohibition, 'You shall not eat,' is replaced by a gracious call addressed to all: 'Come; for all is now ready.'[*] Christ's cross not only plumbs the depth of the knowledge of evil and good; it is truly the tree of *life*, from which God barred our forebears to keep them from lasting forever in listless fallenness.[†] The apparently brutal mercy of death has completed its purpose; the sting of corruption that called for it has been excised from our nature, restored through Christ's sacrifice, death and resurrection to possible innocence. The cross re-admits us to the Garden. A broad perspective opens for humanity in Christ's words to the thief: 'Today you shall be with me in paradise.'[‡]

---

[*] Gen. 2.17; Lk 14.17.
[†] Gen. 3.22.
[‡] Lk. 23.43.

The thought, then, of the cross as tree of life had been alive in Christian consciousness for centuries when the Cistercian movement, to which Arnulf belonged, was founded. However, it enjoyed a resurgence during this same period, the mid-twelfth century, inspiring works of theology and art of sheer magnificence. Pride of place among these belongs to the apse mosaic of San Clemente in Rome, details of which are reproduced on the cover of this book.

The roots of the tree in San Clemente run deep. Contemporary visitors who enter the basilica at street level find themselves on a site that was already a place of worship at about the time when Christ was born. Descending below the present church, into what now resembles a crypt, they find themselves in an earlier Christian basilica constructed in the fourth century, the century of the Council of Nicaea. This in turn is built on top of a first-century Mithraic temple.

In about the year 1100 the lower basilica was no longer thought functional. The street level in Rome had risen. New churches were popping up around the city. The desire arose to ensure that this one would not recede into obscurity. The fourth-century church, stripped of its sacred objects and relics, was filled with rubble. On this foundation the new basilica was built, finished around 1120, just as St Bernard's Clairvaux was consolidating its earliest foundations.

The apse design for this new church was audacious. No mosaic on this scale had been realized in Rome for a couple of centuries. Its fascination is perennial.

At the centre of the mosaic is a cross growing out of what looks like a flowerpot producing a verdant acanthus, the plant that in classical, pre-Christian art stood for immortality. The early Church adopted it as a symbol of resurrection hope. The acanthus sends forth its branches in swirling patterns that fill the apse gloriously, bright green on gold. Various classes of people are enfolded by it, shown to thrive in its embrace. There are clerics and lay people, men and women, farmers and hunters. Every aspect of human existence is touched by the life that extends from the cross. For the apse represents the world, no less, and society in its complex variety.

Animal life is present, too. There are wonderful birds alluding to the parable of the mustard seed: 'When it has grown it is the greatest of shrubs and becomes a tree, so that the birds of the air come and make nests in its branches.'[*] There are dolphins, sheep and goats, proud peacocks and other animals. Each species has potential symbolic worth. The net effect of the ensemble is self-evident: it shows that Christ's redemptive work has a cosmic dimension. No life is untouched by it. Every form of life, in fact, confesses it. We notice this fact when our senses are sufficiently purified. Then we actually perceive that 'the trees of the wood sing for joy'.[†]

The cross is adorned with 12 sparkling doves. Tour guides will tell you they are figures of the apostles sent out to the whole world as messengers of Christ. This is no doubt correct, but our Cistercian reading of the Song of Songs has sensitized us to a further possibility of meaning. Think of the dove cooing 'in the clefts of the rock, in the covert of the

---

[*] Mt. 13.32.
[†] Psalm 96.12.

FLOURISHING

cliff'.[*] Both Bernard and Arnulf see this image fulfilled in Christ's sacred wounds. The doves of San Clemente suggest that the cross can become a familiar roost where it is sweet and safe to perch.

Underneath the cross four rivers run out. The reference points both forward and back. We think at once of the Edenic rivers erupting from paradise at the dawn of creation; of the river Ezekiel saw, flowing from the temple and ensuring that 'everything will live where the river goes'; and of 'the river of the water of life, bright as crystal, flowing from the throne of God and of the Lamb' in Revelation, enabling the tree of life to produce its twelve kinds of fruit and leaves 'for the healing of the nations'.[†] A tiny deer drinks from the rivers' wellspring, unfrightened by the carcass of a serpent that surrounds it. This is to show that mankind's ancient enemy has finally been routed. Two large harts underneath quench their thirst in the flowing streams, recalling the *incipit* of a Psalm that at least since the days of Augustine has been a code for substantiated Christian hope.[‡]

From above celestial light shines. Through layers of illumination the Father's hand emerges holding a victor's crown. The hand bestows on the whole composition upward energy. Creation, shown in its loveliness, is drawn towards

---

[*]Song 2.14.
[†]Gen. 2.10–14; Ezek. 47.9; Rev. 22.1–2.
[‡]'As a hart longs for flowing streams, so longs my soul for thee, O God.' See Psalm 42.1 and Augustine's splendid Enarratio on that Psalm.

a goal beyond itself. 'Our homeland,' we must not forget, 'is in heaven.'*

At first sight the apse of San Clemente may seem to present a sanitized view of Christ's cross, removing its terror, wrapping it in delight. On closer inspection this impression turns out to be false. The central account of crucifixion is realistic. Jesus's wounds are clearly portrayed. Blood pours from his hands, feet, and side. The posture and expression of the Virgin on Christ's right and of the beloved disciple on his left show abject grief. This is no prettified passion scene. It contains the principal elements we have met in Arnulf's pathetic meditation.

Around the cross, nonetheless, a world unfolds that is a world of beauty. It is part of the genius of high medieval art to hold these poles together, bridging the gap. We can confront the central scene without subterfuge and yet be conscious that there is joyful fecundity round about. We can marvel at the pleasantness of life and yet recognize that its goodness is rooted in a mystery of tears.

Believers of earlier centuries accepted tears as a natural component of the Christian condition. Keeping Christ crucified before their eyes, they were alert to signs of the cross in their own circumstances, equipped to confront these in truth while imbuing them with the light-filled hope sprung from faith. A modern sensibility is more apt to seek pure consolation in religion and to make us feel let down when comfort is not found straight away. In so far as

---

*Phil. 3.20.

we cry at all, do our tears not tend to be tears of self-pity rather than tears of compassion?

I have in the last few years been helped to reflect on this question of tears by a text discovered in Norway's first printed book, the *Missale Nidrosiense*, published in 1519 at the behest of the penultimate archbishop of Nidaros, medieval Trondheim, Erik Valkendorf (1465–1522). Two years before the Missal was printed, Luther had published his 95 theses. Christian Europe was in ferment. Valkendorf smelt the storm brewing, but was not blown about by winds of doctrine. He stood up to power, resolved to renew and beautify the Church from within. This work, he knew, must be grounded in prayer. The commissioning of a new missal and breviary for his vast metropolis, extending beyond Norway to the North of Scotland and down to the Isle of Man, was part of this overall enterprise. One of the first prayers in Valkendorf's Missal is specific to it. At least, I have not found its equivalent anywhere else. It is set as an obligatory formula to be recited by all the priests of the metropolis each time they are about to offer Mass. It runs like this:

Da mihi, domine, lachrimas internas, que peccatorum meorum possint soluere maculas et celesti iocunditate semper repleant animam meam. Rogo te, Iesu, per benignissimas lachrimas tuas, vt des mihi gratiam lachrimarum, quam sine dono tuo non possum habere; da mihi fontem irriguum lachrimarum, vt sint mihi lachrime mee panes die ac nocte. Prepara hanc mensam famulo tuo in conspectu tuo et da mihi eam in potestatem vt quotiens volo satier ex ea.

Grant me, Lord, inward tears with strength to cleanse the stains of my sins and fill my soul with heavenly gladness always. I pray you, Jesus, by your own most kind tears:

grant me the grace of tears which, apart from your gift, is beyond me. Grant me a fountain of tears that will not dry up, that my tears may be my bread by day and by night. Prepare this table for your servant in your sight that it may strengthen me. I desire to eat my fill of it daily.[*]

Who, these days, would come up with such a prayer? Our modern understanding of tears is one-dimensional, arrested in sentiment. Such are not the tears intended here.

The Fathers, wary of self-indulgence, frowned upon outbursts of emotion. The tears which Christians of old aspired to cry were other, having much in common with the *lacrimae rerum* of Virgil. When Aeneas recalled the blood shed at Troy, he cried out, in W. F. J. Knight's paraphrase, 'The world has tears as a constituent part of it, and so have our own lives hopeless and weary.'[†] The 'tears of things' acknowledge illusionlessly that this world, in its brittle beauty, is broken.

Jesus's 'most kind tears' were tears of this sort, I would say. The verse 'Jesus wept' occurs in the story of the raising of Lazarus. Reproached by Martha for arriving too late, the Lord is taken to the tomb. Seeing Mary and her company approach disconsolate, Jesus, 'deeply moved in spirit', weeps in turn.[‡]

Preachers cite this passage to speak of Christ's affection and to point towards the hallowing of ours. The point is

---

[*]The *Missale Nidrosiense* is available online at <www.bokselskap.no/boker/missale>.
[†]Cf. Aeneid, 1.461–2. Knight's phrase is found in his *Roman Vergil* (London: Faber & Faber, 1944), p. 193.
[‡]Jn 11.20–35.

valid. The evidence is unsure. From the outset, Jesus says: 'This illness is not unto death; it is for the glory of God.'[*] He knew what he would do. He doubted not his competence to do it. The raising of Lazarus would be the final 'sign' pointing forward to his own resurrection. It makes no sense that Christ should weep, at this moment of 'glory', for one about to be restored to life.

That it was not in the evangelist's mind to suggest it appears from the verse: 'The Jews said: "See how he loved him."'[†] Throughout John's account, 'the Jews', that is, 'the gawpers, not the followers', *all* the Gospel's protagonists, including its Hero, being Jews, are assigned a specific role: they get the wrong end of the stick. This serves a pedagogic purpose. Proffering mistaken or limited views, they draw forth from the Word made flesh a fuller revelation. That they ascribe Christ's tears to affection for his friend suggests that something quite different is at stake.

Indeed, what causes Christ to weep is the sight of humanity weeping. His tears show him aggrieved, indignant at the scandal of death's reign in beings made for immortality, who long for paradise lost and lost friendship. Having wept, he goes up to Calvary to work our redemption. Priests do well, certainly, to weep likewise on ascending to the altar where Christ's sacrifice remains present and effective.

By virtue of this sacrifice, our tears are transformed. They are imbued with a 'heavenly gladness' that does not cancel grief, but makes of grief its receptacle. It is hard to talk about

---

[*] Jn 11.4.
[†] Jn 11.36.

this. Language ordinarily labours to define opposites, not to at-one them. Visual art, like the San Clemente mosaic, stands a better chance, for it can juxtapose contrasting realities. Poetry, like Arnulf's, also helps, gracing speech with the polyvalence of music. Ultimately, though, we must inhabit this mystery in silence. Only in the hush of our inner sanctuary, a room many people spend a lifetime avoiding, can we know Christ's gift intimately. There he strikes our heart's rock with the wood of the vivifying tree, provoking tears of adoration. 'Through the wood', we sing on Good Friday, 'joy entered the world'.[*] Victory is won through defeat; a crucified body frees us. To take all this in, we are invited to enter a uniquely Christian condition of reconciled contradiction. The Father liked to call this state *charmolupē*, a 'sadness-gladness'. It produces mournful–joyful tears.

Our Paschal proclamation is not 'Hurrah!' The Easter Vigil's Alleluia sounds hesitant at first. Intoned by a single voice, it hardly dares credit the message with which it is entrusted. The first believers' response to the empty tomb was of 'trembling and *ekstasis*': they were outside themselves.[†] From that weird vantage point, they had to reconsider all things, gains and losses, graces and sins.

To find one's place in a world made new is a gigantic proposition.

When Erik Valkendorf had his Missal produced in a Paris printery, the order of the world as he knew it was

---

[*] 'Ecce enim propter lignum venit gaudium in universo mundo', an acclamation introducing the Improperia.
[†] Mk 16.8.

floundering. Rooting his people's devotion in tears, he relieved them of overly simplified notions of hope. Trauma in response to disaster often stems from the unbiblical fiction that the world is, and ought to be experienced as, all right. To declare it instead sick, 'a vale of tears', is not pessimistic.* It is to own that the world needs saving still; that Easter is not a past event, but present; that our life, our joy and hope depend on it. Only in paradise, when we are home at last, *with* Jesus, will God make all crying cease. For now, we eat our fill from his table as wanderers, his bread seasoned with our tears.

The *Rhythmica oratio* is concerned to lodge meditation on Jesus's medicinal wounds in our heart. To pursue this meditation serenely is to learn to synthesize varied experience. It is to re-weave our life as a seamless whole according to a perfect pattern instead of leaving it a stitched-up patchwork. Christ is our peace. When he, crucified and risen, lives in our heart and rules there, we can confront trial *in* peace and become in the midst of it peacemakers for others.† Pain born patiently can, in Hopkins's memorable phrase, plume to peace over time, like a chick that grows from a shivering lump of bony flesh into a gracious wood dove.‡ Faith does not take our pain away, but shows a use for it; it endows it with finality.

---

*Cf. the phrase 'in hac lacrimarum valle' of the Salve Regina, which Cistercians sing each evening, all year round, at Compline, before going to bed.
†Cf. Eph. 2.14; Col. 3.15; Mt. 5.9.
‡See the poem 'Peace' that begins, 'When will you, Peace, wild wooddove'.

The wounds of Christ crucified, by which the world is saved, stay open. Our wounds, configured to his, can likewise become sources of grace for ourselves and others even while we await eventual, perfect restoration to full health.

The medieval Cistercians kept Christ crucified in mind and heart by means of stories cited from the Church's patrimony. A thirteenth-century collection of such stories compiled in a northern French abbey cites a legend about an ancient martyr named Nimias. Urged by a pagan tyrant to renounce his faith, Nimias said he could not, in as much as Christ lived in his heart. The tyrant asked for him to be disembowelled and for his 'whole heart to be pulled out and cut open, so that he might see whether Christ was indeed within it, as the martyr claimed'. When this was done,

> there appeared in the middle of his opened heart a most beautiful effigy of the Crucified, stretching through the length and breadth of his heart. When he saw this, the tyrant blushed. The crowd of the faithful, meanwhile, exulted greatly on account of such a miracle. They stretched out their hands to heaven while they knelt on the ground and shouted for joy, with tears, to the Lord, saying: 'Glory to you, Lord, for letting us so magnificently put to the test the truth of what your apostle says about Christ dwelling in our hearts through faith.'[*]

---

[*] *Collectio exemplorum Cisterciensis in codice Parisiensis 15912 asseruata*, ed. Jacques Berlioz, Marie Anne Polo de Beaulieu and others, *Corpus Christianorum, Continuatio Medievalis*, 243 (Turnhout: Brepols, 2012), p. 264.

The collection from which this story comes circulated widely. It was written up during Abbot Arnulf's lifetime in a monastery not far from his, of the same Order. Would he have believed in the literal truth of the tyrant's find? He may not have excluded it. Principally, though, I think he would have found in this tale an imaged summary of his poetic effort, which aims to teach us what life in Christ is *like*, what it means to have his cross lodged in our heart, to put on his mind, to give our life for our friends, to love unconditionally.

As we begin to learn this new way of living, we find that our tears can coexist with heartfelt joy. We see reality differently.

What does this mean in practice?

Shortly before my solemn profession as a monk, an acquaintance sent me a note to wish me well. She enclosed a photograph. It showed, she explained, a fresco she was fond of from the crypt of Chevetogne, an abbey founded in Belgium a century ago, some 60 kilometres, as the crow flies, south of the ruins of Arnulf's Villers. The photograph disturbed me. It showed a man in a monastic habit nailed to a cross. The legend, in Greek, read simply, 'The Crucified Monk'. The scene displays the reality of spiritual battle. The monk is pierced by arrows and nails of temptation to be endured in communion with Christ's royal combat on Calvary.

I could see the pertinence of this reminder. I needed to galvanize my resolve. Still, what kind of a picture was this to send a young man preparing with rejoicing to consecrate his future?

Only when I turned the photograph over and read the inscription on the back did I get the point. 'This,' it was written in ballpoint, 'is the image of a man so fully configured to Christ that he no longer contemplates him on the cross from afar, but sees the world through the eyes of Christ crucified.' This perspective, at once demanding and enchanting, had never occurred to me before. I was at once convinced of its truth. It still orients my existence.

Our wounds will finally heal when they have become so one with Christ's, so fully surrendered, that we no longer know where his passion ends and ours begins. We are caught up, then, in the inexorable victory of his life over our death, of his light over our darkness, of his wholeness over our fragmentation. United with him in death, we are drawn into his life, over which human mortality and sickness have no power. The process takes time. The anguish is real before the prospect of broadness opens. But sooner or later we no longer look into the darkness of the cleft in which the dove hides, but out of it. We see, then, a world infinitely loved, transfigured, worthy to *be* loved. Peering out from the dove's nest, we perceive that

> the winter is past,
> > the rain is over and gone.
> The flowers appear on the earth,
> > the time of singing has come,
> and the voice of the turtledove
> > is heard in our land.
> The fig tree puts forth its figs,
> > and the vines are in blossom;
> > they give forth fragrance.

We hear the Beloved call to us: 'Arise, my love, my fair one, and come away.'*

We who sow at times with weeping, at a loss, shall return home with shouts of joy, bearing fragrant golden sheaves.† Even seed sown on rock is fruitful where there are tiny fissures. A wound in the rock face is what it takes for life to take hold and so, at the opportune time, to bear fruit thirtyfold, sixtyfold, a hundredfold, a harvest for the feeding of multitudes.‡

When Christ at Easter appeared to Mary Magdalene, Apostle to the Apostles, it was in a garden.§ There he awaits us also. His wounds remain, but they are glorified. The death-tree has become the tree of predilection. Poison has turned into a cure. The message of the wounded-and-victorious One is: 'Peace!'¶

By his wounds we are healed. By ours we learn what it means to be loved and saved, commissioned to carry Christ's fruitful work forward in compassion.

---

*Song 2.11–13.
†Psalm 126.6.
‡Mt. 13.18–23.
§Jn 20.11–18.
¶Jn 20.19.

ET LVCERNÆ
ARDENTES IN MA
NIBVS VESTRIS.
POSVI ORI
MEO CVSTO
DIAM
SPES MEA
DESCENDE
DE CRVCE
GENVA MEA INFIR
MATA SVNT A IEIVNIO
ABOMNI VIA MALA
PROHIBVI PEDES MEOS.
PAVPER
TAS

I saw this wall painting in the Cistercian abbey of Mogiła, near Nowa Huta, a long time after I received the photograph of the fresco in Chevetogne. I was moved to find the same motif in a familiar setting. This image, painted in a Western style, picks up the themes of the Oriental icon. The monk here wears a Cistercian cowl. His broad heart is unencumbered, determinedly vulnerable. It has become, as you can see, an open book. By remaining on the cross that Providence assigns to him he is a point of stability for others. In the midst of commotion, he radiates peace. The immeasurable riches of Christ Jesus are manifest in his wounded poverty, the white rose of 'Paupertas' blooming at his feet. From it his self-oblation in charity arises.

Notes on the Text

Biblical quotations are taken, on the whole, from the Revised Standard Version. Unless otherwise noted, translations of other texts are mine.

I am grateful to Sister Mary Thomas Brown, the Carmelites of Ware, Dom Elias Dietz, Father Iakovos Kiziridis, Father Theodosios Martzouchos and Abbot Xavier Perrin for helpful exchanges. I thank Robin Baird-Smith for commissioning the book.

My version of the *Rhythmica oratio* is based on the Latin text in Migne's *Patrologia Latina*, volume CLXXXIV. I have made a couple of minor adjustments, filling in a missing syllable here, a lacking word there; changing an '*amoenus*' (which makes no sense) to '*amarus*'. A modern critical edition, however, has not yet been produced. One can only hope that renewed interest in this lovely work will provoke one.

I first developed my reading of Erik Valkendorf's prayer for tears in an article in *The Tablet*. The material is reproduced here with the gracious consent of the editor.

Each of the poem's seven parts consists of ten stanzas except the one '*Ad cor*', which has 14. Does the total number of 74 have symbolic significance? In the Book of Exodus, we are told that 74 Israelites ascended Sinai and saw the Lord God: 'there was under his feet as it were a pavement of sapphire stone, like the very heaven for clearness. And he did not lay his hand on the chief men of the people of Israel; they beheld God, and ate and drank' (Exodus 24.9–11). Whether this coincidence is deliberate I dare not say; but I would not rule it out, given Abbot Arnulf's biblical culture and his concern to present Christ's wounds as epiphanic and eucharistic.

I finished writing this book on the feast of Saints Peter and Paul 2024. That same day my father died. I dedicate *Healing Wounds* to his memory and that of my mother.

> *Pie Iesu Domine, dona eis requiem.*
> *Tantus labor non sit cassus.*